America in the Movies

AMERICA IN THE MOVIES

OR

"Santa Maria, It Had Slipped My Mind"

MICHAEL WOOD

Columbia University Press
New York

Columbia University Press Morningside Edition
New York   Oxford
Copyright © 1975 by Basic Books, Inc.
Morningside Edition with New Preface copyright © 1989
by Columbia University Press

Library of Congress Cataloging-in-Publication Data

Wood, Michael, 1936–
America in the movies,
or, "Santa Maria, it had slipped my mind".
Reprint. Originally published: New York ; Basic Books, 1975.
Includes index.
1. Motion pictures—California—Los Angeles—History.
2. Hollywood (Los Angeles, Calif.)—History.
3. United States in motion pictures.   I. Title.
PN1993.5.U65W6   1989   791.43'6273   89-9969
ISBN 0-231-07098-5 (alk. paper)
ISBN 0-231-07099-3 (pbk. : alk. paper)

Casebound editions of Columbia University Press books are Smyth-sewn
and are printed on permanent and durable acid-free paper
∞
Printed in the United States of America

p 10 9 8 7 6 5 4 3

For my mother and father
and their memories of Ronald Colman

CONTENTS

ILLUSTRATIONS   ix
PREFACE TO THE MORNINGSIDE EDITION   xi
ACKNOWLEDGMENTS   xxi

I

The Price of Imagery   3

II

America First   24

III

The Blame on Mame   51

IV

Nice Guys Finish Last   75

CONTENTS

V

The Intrepidation of Dreams   97

VI

Ceremonies of Innocence   126

VII

Darkness in the Dance   146

VIII

Shake the Superflux   165

IX

The Sense of the Past   189

INDEX   197

ILLUSTRATIONS

Tyrone Power and Linda Darnell in *The Mark of Zorro* — 5

Marlene Dietrich in *Touch of Evil* — 7

John Garfield and Eleanor Parker in *Pride of the Marines* — 41

Robert Taylor and Richard Widmark in *The Law and Jake Wade* — 45

Rita Hayworth in *Gilda* — 53

Marilyn Monroe in *Some Like It Hot* — 73

Glenn Ford in *The Fastest Gun Alive* — 83

Paul Newman in *The Hustler* — 89

Jack Carson and Zachary Scott in *Mildred Pierce* — 105

Cary Grant and Joan Fontaine in *Suspicion* — 115

Dana Andrews in *The Ox-Bow Incident* — 137

Robert Ryan in *Crossfire* — 139

Gene Kelly in *Singin' in the Rain* — 157

Gene Kelly in *It's Always Fair Weather* — 159

The Ten Commandments — 171

Samson and Delilah — 179

Marlon Brando in *The Wild One* — 191

PREFACE TO THE
MORNINGSIDE EDITION

I suppose we scarcely ever fully focus our readers, even when writing quite ordinary letters. The reader becomes a spectre, kinder or harsher than life; or a mere outline, half-hidden in mists of anxiety or longing. I certainly didn't have a single sort of reader in mind for this book, didn't directly think much at all about a readership; but I did have a sense of a small crowd of potential critics hovering somewhere just off the edge of my vision. They were not an unfriendly group, but they were very tough and very skeptical, and they knew a lot more about movies than I did—they had seen more movies, and they knew more about the movie business. Or they knew even less than I did, and were skeptical for quite different reasons—they didn't like flimsy generalizations, thought you couldn't really talk about the movies in the way that I was proposing.

My actual readers, as far as I can tell from reviews, correspondence, conversations, hearsay, were far less suspicious, more sympathetic to speculation, willing to take all kinds of chances: altogether a more attractive bunch. When they didn't like the book it was not because they were skeptics but because they were believers, to whom *my* skepticism seemed frivolity, a failure to take the movies seriously. A friend and colleague shocked me by saying the book was fine except for its anti-intellectual streak. That was not what I meant at all, but I knew at once what she was saying. I had been anxious not to drop names and pontificate, and my attempts at discretion and my all too bearable lightness of touch looked like embarrassment. They only looked like it, though; and I hope only sometimes.

If I had been writing a little later than 1974, the names I did (quietly) drop, those of Lévi-Strauss and Althusser, for example, would have raised the question of theory, and where I stood. I took it for granted, a bit naively no doubt, that one couldn't think of the relation of film and society without some sort of theory in mind, but that the practice of the theory, what the theory looked like when it was working, was the interesting thing. My imaginary readers made me a little nervous about saying this; my real (and new) readers may perhaps be grateful if I now try to come clean.

I accept the notion of "ideology" as sketched out by Althusser in a quotation late in the book; and I associate it with Foucault's vision of what he calls the conditions of possibility of knowledge, the historical framework of what at any given time is thinkable. I picture Althusser's "world" and Foucault's "configurations" as marked by a horizon, and movies as one of the ways in which a culture constitutes its horizon, tells itself what it can't see beyond. More important for my purposes, movies are a crucial mode by which a culture thinks through and about the world this side of the horizon. For the period of American history reflected in the book, roughly the 1940s and 1950s, the horizon remained steady—or at least steady enough to be considered the same horizon. In the 1930s and 1960s, I suggest, the horizons were rather different, and require different instruments for their inspection.

In Lévi-Strauss I discovered the concept of neurosis as an individual myth, and myth as a collective neurosis; the myth enacting an imaginary solution to an authentic dilemma. The elegance of this theory is that the solution *has* to be imaginary *because* the dilemma is authentic—if there were a real solution, the myth wouldn't be needed. In my own, looser version of this proposition, movies deal in fragments of myth rather than fully articulated stories, and the fragments don't have to solve the dilemma, only to exercise it, give it a run. I would say now that they need to negotiate it, in the way a car negotiates a bend (Barthes' analogy) or the way negotiations and love songs, as Paul Simon says, are often mistaken for one and the same.

The place of these negotiations is what I called, in a familiar, almost worn-away idiom, the back of the mind. I have found this hypothetical location more and more useful over the years, since it seems crowded with all kinds of activity. It is, I reckon, one of popular culture's great arenas, the zone where we habitually chase and then lose our questions about what entertainment is and what it is for. Other metaphors would do as well, of course; but they would all have to evoke a realm at the edge of consciousness or language—the tip of the tongue, say, which is the same scene given a more anatomical coloring. This apparently marginal realm turns out to be littered with our central concerns; yet it can't be the unconscious in any serious psychoanalytic sense because the material in it is more like an itch than a trauma, not confronted but not repressed. Many cultural contradictions can be openly acknowledged, and sometimes are. But often they are not. They are tucked away from conscious thought, hidden in representations, so that we think of them without thinking, exactly as we often continue to worry at matters we have officially banished from our minds. From the front and middle of our minds, that is. They are lingering somewhere, or we wouldn't be worried.

Empson's idea of ambiguity may also be a source for this argument, along with his remarks about Fielding's irony in *Tom Jones*. The word "prudence," for example, works for Fielding in the way myths work for Lévi-Strauss' Brazilian Indians and the way I see fragments of myth working in Hollywood movies. Prudence is desirable and difficult, but also dodgy, even despicable. It is not a question of Fielding's showing us, in some flat, didactic way, which kind of prudence is the right kind, but of his testing the word empirically on his readers, in the world; of his investigating the word's reach, the actual stretch of the contradictions we need it to cover. Humphrey Bogart's face does something of the same sort for loneliness.

One of my reviewers, well disposed to the book but inclined to think it all pretty lightweight, spoke of my having a "grasshopper mind." This amused my family a lot, and the image became our catchphrase for all rapid or unmodulated changes of subject. Of course, I wouldn't want to promote grasshopping as an intellectual habit, and I myself feel there are quite a few places in this book where I should have stayed with an argument rather than moving so swiftly on. But I also feel the hopping has some merits. I wanted to show that American myths in the movies were often intricate and deep, mostly casual and yet closely linked to one another, a sort of tangled tapestry, and for this I needed to travel at some speed among them. You could bump into myths at every turn, was my suggestion, and into far more myths than I could explore.

There is one particularly wild piece of grasshopping which I couldn't resist at the time and can't regret now. It concerns not another myth in the movies but the recurring conspiracy of what I call the children of optics, the taunting play of movies with appearances, which are their chief language but also their mask and their mystery. A further figure for this topic might have been the scene in *Duck Soup* where Harpo impersonates Groucho in the empty space which Groucho takes to be a mirror. Visually there is no difference between the Harpo/Groucho we see and the Groucho we might have seen if the mirror had been intact. Until, for example, Groucho spins round but Harpo doesn't, remaining nevertheless in a posture which exactly reflects Groucho's when he turns again to face him. This, it seems to me, is how movies work: we are Groucho at the (absent) mirror, what we see is all there is and far from enough. We have our suspicions but only our suspicions. We build a fictional world out of all we see and all we don't see. Except that here we are shown precisely the difference that is denied to Groucho: a zany metaphor for what we usually do not know. We have magically gone behind appearances, when everyone knows that in film the only place behind appearances is the set. But then we need to remember that Harpo dressed as Groucho is not reality but yet another appearance, and the dizzying question perhaps is not what is real in such representations, but whether appearances ever end and how we distinguish among them. Foucault might have done even more with *Duck Soup* than he did with *Las Meninas*.

At the beginning of this book I try to evoke my own relation to the movies I discuss, and the evocation looms a little larger than it probably should. I wanted to suggest that these movies were very much alive for me, a continuing pleasure, since I had seen them all, again or for the first time, in the 1970s; but also that their home was in history, that they were no longer strictly contemporary. Of course the movies would have exhibited just the same features and preoccupations even had I felt quite differently about them, and I was seeking to make what turns out to be a double critical point, not seen as double at the time.

First, Hollywood films of the 1940s and 1950s were a *world*, and moviegoers became vicarious natives of it, connoisseurs of its habits and fauna and scenery. This perception is obvious enough, and had been for a long time before I was writing, but it is important nonetheless. Movies of other periods have not always made a world; and it is the sense of a world that allows us to think purposefully about the myths these movies purvey. All their implications have other implications.

Second, this world characteristically dealt in the sort of exaggerated gesture, verbal or visual or narrative, which my subtitle illustrates, and which might seem an obstacle to our taking its concerns seriously. This point is a more complicated one, and logically only very loosely connected to the first. Movies could be a world and not be overblown at all, and they could be overblown without being a world. I was trying to suggest, I think, that the moral and stylistic excesses of these movies were a language like that of popular songs or verbal cliché. This language is the only one many people have, and in any case has all kinds of subtleties of its own, reasons of the heart which the higher flying reason knows nothing of. García Márquez seems to mean something similar when he says *One Hundred Years of Solitude* is "like a bolero"; and his *Love in the Time of Cholera is* a bolero, a patient exploration of a sentimental history.

So I was not apologizing for old films or the pleasure they gave me, but trying to point to certain qualities in them. Without some such feeling for the movies, it seems to me, we can't make any sense at all of *Casablanca* or *Gone with the Wind*, or thousands of other productions.

My claim was too general, though, since it seemed to imply that all Hollywood films need to be viewed in this way. In fact, many Hollywood films are not overblown at all. They have conventions and we need to know how they work, but the same is true of *Paradise Lost*. There are no excesses, no Santa Marias or hearts pounding like cannonfire, in films like *Gilda* and *The Hustler* and dozens of austere westerns. It is absurd, perhaps, to say as I do that *The Hustler* is "a very great movie" ("If *The Hustler* is a great movie," F. W. Dupee once growled to me, "what are we going to call *Battleship Potemkin?*"); but it and many other Hollywood features are very good movies, major works of popular art. They set their own terms of reference and they meet them. They don't invite the complicity of our smile, and I find I don't write about them as if they did.

There is another implication of my claim, not intended but hardly deniable, and best formulated by Luke Menand, who says that (along with Stanley Cavell) I find in the very commercialism of older Hollywood movies the guarantee of a sort of integrity. They have the grace not to pretend to be high art. Cavell praises *The Awful Truth* but calls *Citizen Kane* a bag of tricks; I delight in *Gone with the Wind* and *Casablanca* but complain (although not in this book) about *Apocalypse Now*. "What sort of critical standard is it," Menand wonders, "that allows David O. Selznick to go about gilding the biggest lilies he can find, but asks Francis Coppola to keep *The Golden Bough* out of his movie about Vietnam?" The shaky sort. I could half-evade the charge by saying that my point is critical but not primarily evaluative, that I am trying to distinguish among movies rather than rate them. But evaluation lurks in my descriptions all the same, and I do suggest that the overblown, in its place, is "just right." A better answer would return us to my sense of the older movies as a world, and insist that worlds change. It is also true that different movies are overblown in quite different ways, that the exaggerations of *Apocalypse Now* are not those of *Gone with the Wind*. This is not a matter of integrity but of perceived result. Coppola, toward the end of his movie, tries hard for the highbrow effect and misses; Selznick tries throughout for the broad middlebrow effect and, given the broadness of the brow, could hardly not get it.

Still, I agree with Menand that there are contexts in which we would want to say that *Apocalypse Now*, with its faults, is a better movie than *Gone with the Wind*, with all its successes, and it may be less a matter of my allowing to Selznick what I won't allow to Coppola than of my making of Coppola demands I don't make of Selznick. A double standard? well, a multiple standard—a standard multiplied by as many *kinds* of movie as we are trying to make sense of. This is scrappy, I'm afraid, but we are looking at scrappy ground, and the principle surely is as far as possible to let the movies themselves set the standards by which we judge them.

As for the innocence that Cavell and I both claim to have lost in our relation to the movies, this now strikes me as hocus pocus. It's not that we didn't have the innocence or that we didn't lose it, it's that the innocence doesn't matter either way. We don't write any better about the movies for having it or not having it, and it introduces all kinds of distractions into an already untidy region. I'm glad

Cavell's name has come up, though, because it gives me a chance to say something about my rather churlish mentions of him in this book, where I rarely evoke him except to disagree. The disagreements are real enough, but their expression conveys very little of my grateful and continuing sense of dialogue. I was delighted when a sensitive reviewer, David Bromwich, spotted nevertheless how grateful the dialogue was.

Quite a few writers, I guess, find out what they want to say only after they have said it, but some of us are *very* slow—I began to understand one of the chief drifts of this book about a year after it was published. It wasn't that I reread the thing or actively rethought it, rather that certain concerns seeped slowly out into a kind of clarity.

I was fairly sure from the start that the movie images I explored had something to do with the American history of the time, but I wasn't sure how they added up, and I wasn't brave enough to insist on the connections I hoped for. The year's seepage suggested to me that the images really did hang together quite well; that Humphrey Bogart, Rita Hayworth, power-haunted westerns, class-colored thrillers, problem pictures, Gene Kelly dancing, epic crowds on the march—the list and the book could have been extended—formed a composite but coherent picture of an aspect of America at a particular time.

It was a portrait not of an anxious nation pretending to be confident, as is often said of the America of the period, and as I blandly suggest in my chapter on musicals, but of the anxieties of a still confident nation; of a confidence that was cracking but still substantial, going but not gone. It was a portrait of American bewilderment, but also of an energetic refusal of complication and helplessness. Not an easy period to characterize simply, and of course these generalizations are not the story, only pointers to it. The story is in the details, in the sight of particular movies negotiating particular dilemmas; and we confirm (or deny) this story not by surveying the conscious responses of moviegoers or by setting hard historical fact against mere fiction, but by finding (failing to find) instances of these movie mentalities, these modes of facing and not facing nagging issues, elsewhere in American life. When Hugh Brogan tells us that Roosevelt for a long time "would not allow foreign policy considerations of any kind to interfere with his domestic programme," this is not a model for life in Rick's Café in Casablanca before the arrival of Ingrid Bergman, it is a sign that Rick and Roosevelt share a horizon, inhabit the same worried world and resort to similar tactics for keeping it at bay. In this sense the movies are not so much a mirror as a sort of historical stethoscope. We hear heart murmurs through them; some already heard, some pretty unexpected.

ACKNOWLEDGMENTS

A GREAT many thoughts in this book have appeared, in one form or another, in *New Society*, and I am very grateful to Paul Barker, editor of *New Society*, for giving me a regular chance to stumble upon them. My thanks, too, to Judy Brown, Barbara Uribe, Carol Vance, Maurice Hatton, James Price, and Jonathan Steinberg for ideas, information, help, skepticism, and intelligence.

Portions of my essay, "Movie Crazy," are found in Chapter I. (Reprinted with permission from *The New York Review of Books*, November 29, 1973. Copyright © 1973 by Nyrev, Inc.)

An excerpt from my review of Fred Lawrence Guiles's *Norma Jean* appears in Chapter III. (Reprinted from *Commentary*, September 1969, by permission. Copyright © 1969 by the American Jewish Committee.)

I have also drawn on my articles "When the Music Stops" and "Unflinching, Sort of," which originally appeared in *The Columbia Forum*, Volume 1, Spring 1972 and Volume 3, Fall 1974, respectively.

Finally, I am grateful for permission to quote from the following copyrighted material: *Memo from David O. Selznick*, selected and edited by Rudy Behlmer. Copyright © 1972 by Selznick Properties, Ltd. Reprinted by permission of the Viking Press, Inc. and Macmillan, London and Basingstoke.

America in the Movies

I

The Price of Imagery

For ignorance is the first requisite of the historian. . . .

Lytton Strachey,
Eminent Victorians

If now all of this is to be turned into a dream, the psychical material will be submitted to a pressure which will condense it greatly, to an internal fragmentation and displacement which will, as it were, create new surfaces. . . .

Sigmund Freud,
On Dreams

TYRONE POWER is a dashing young cadet at the Madrid military academy. We see him excelling on horseback and at sword practice, and at the end of a busy morning of demonstrating his prowess, he is approached by a fellow student, who says, "Have you forgotten that you are to cross swords with Captain Fulano at three o'clock this afternoon?" Power slaps his forehead theatrically with the flat of his hand, and says, "Santa Maria, it had slipped my mind." The gesture and the exclamation would be ludicrous in a play or a novel, and would be comic in a film of any serious pretensions. Where they are, though, in Rouben Mamoulian's *The Mark of Zorro* (1940), they are perfect, just what is needed. We may smile, but we don't laugh. If we do smile, it is partly, no doubt, because we feel that whatever life was like at the Madrid military academy in the last century, it cannot have been like this; yet we smile mainly because we feel that this is what life is always like in the movies: stylishly overdone.

Or mawkishly overdone. In Edmund Goulding's *Till We Meet Again* (1940), Merle Oberon, a rich young girl with a heart condition, meets George Brent, a convicted murderer temporarily separated from his escort, in a bar in Hong Kong. It is love at first drink. They smash the tops of their glasses and lay the stems, crossed, on the bar. On their way back to America by boat, they are out on the deck one night, coat collars up, swathed in romantic mist. Oberon says, "I could talk to you forever." Brent says, "Will you? Talk to me . . . forever?" "Forever," she repeats thoughtfully, clearly brooding about her heart and her brief life. And he says, "There's always forever," meaning that only in some other, eternal existence will they get a chance to stay together. They agree to meet in Mexico, and sure enough, as the film ends, with Oberon dead of her heart condition and Brent gone to the electric chair, we see a lively New Year's party in Mexico. We hear the sound of glasses smashing, and two stems lie crossed on the bar: there is no one there.

Or morally oversold. Gene Kelly, in Busby Berkeley's *For Me and My Gal* (1942), breaks his hand in order to stay

The Mark of Zorro (1940): The fight for love and glory—Tyrone Power and Linda Darnell strike the perfect movie pose. Courtesy of Twentieth Century-Fox. © 1940 Twentieth Century-Fox Film Corporation. All Rights Reserved.

in vaudeville and out of the army during World War I. Judy Garland doesn't take kindly to this, since her brother has just been killed in action, and she tells Kelly, "You'll never make the big time because you're small time in your heart." Humbled and abandoned, Kelly now tries desperately to get into the war, and ends up heroically driving through a German barrage with a message, and destroying a machine gun emplacement for good measure. But not before he has met up with Garland in Paris, and told her that the only medal he wants is her respect. "My only claim to fame," he says, groveling: "you were once my girl."

It is all too much—overplayed, overwritten—and it is all just right. The good moments of many movies have the flavor of old jokes told a bit too broadly. They are full-blown, as Gavin Lambert says of a sunset in *Gone With The Wind* (1939), but not overblown. Or rather, they are overblown, but that's the way they should be.

André Bazin once wrote that Chaplin is not sentimental, he just seems sentimental to literary people because in a book he would be sentimental. This is not always true, since *Limelight* (1952) is maudlin by any standards, but it is true for *Modern Times* (1936), say, which feels sentimental when you think about it but isn't when you see it. The same sort of argument applies to many good moments in movies: they would be grotesque in another medium. I don't mean that one can't overdo things in the movies—merely that the movies have a measure of their own for how much is enough. Remember Welles's abuse of long, raking camera angles, and of shots for which he obviously had a cameraman crawling at an actor's feet; Hitchcock's taste for naturally overproduced locations like Mount Rushmore; the voices visiting Vivien Leigh at the end of

Touch of Evil (1957): Too much style is just enough—Marlene Dietrich about to tell Orson Welles's bleak future. Culver Pictures.

Gone With The Wind, urging her to go back to Tara; Bogart in *Casablanca* (1943), telling Ingrid Bergman what he recalls of their last day in Paris ("I remember every detail. The Germans wore gray, you wore blue"); Bogart again, telling Claude Rains in the same film that he came to Casablanca for the waters ("Waters?" Rains says. "What waters? We're in the desert." Bogart: "I was misinformed"); Welles again in *Touch of Evil* (1957), asking Marlene Dietrich to tell his future (Dietrich looks at him sourly from beneath hooded lids, and says, "You don't have any").

This sense of the overblown is not a question of hindsight or changing tastes, of our finding ironies and wit where contemporary audiences saw only slices of life. Nor is it a question of such movies being aimed at a split-level audience of sophisticates and groundlings. It is a question of the exact tone of these movies, of their being simultaneously hammed up and just right, pitched at their own chosen level of swagger and exaggeration. There is no irony there, just a modest excess of style; and this, it seems to me, is something like Hollywood's signature in the cinema. This is not life, the signature says, and it is not art, not realism, not even fantasy. It is *the movies*, an independent universe, self-created, self-perpetuating, a licensed zone of unreality, affectionately patronized by us all, the only place in the world where anyone says, "Santa Maria, it had slipped my mind."

It is also a perfectly predictable place, and this is another familiar response to the movies. When Tyrone Power says the duel has slipped his mind, we all know we are not going to see the duel. There hasn't been enough preparation, and we interpret the cue as we are meant to:

as an illustration of the sort of life Power is leading in old Madrid. The real business of the film is elsewhere (in old California, as it happens). On the other hand, we also know that the dialogue I quoted from *Till We Meet Again* is virtually a death warrant. People who have talked like this to each other are doomed; their happy end is bound to be beyond the veil. Similarly, when Gene Kelly tells Judy Garland that the only medal he wants is her respect, most moviegoers know at once that he'll get half a dozen real medals as well, because he has earned them by being so modest and so penitent. After such a line, it would hardly be fair to leave him with her respect alone.

I am thinking of a particular kind of movie, of course. Of Hollywood movies in a particular period. I don't wish to deny that these movies mirror reality in all kinds of ways. On the contrary, this book is a session at the mirror. But I do want to suggest that Hollywood movies, from the end of the 1930s to the beginning of the 1960s, from *Gone With The Wind*, say, to *Cleopatra* (1963), were a *world* in the sense that the novels of Balzac were a world.. They were a system of assumptions and beliefs and preoccupations, a fund of often interchangeable plots, characters, patches of dialogue, and sets. Literally interchangeable at times. "Much of Shangri-La," Reyner Banham says in his book on Los Angeles,

had to be built in three dimensions, the spiral ramps of the production numbers of Busby Berkeley musical spectaculars had to support the weight of a hundred girls in silver top hats, and so on. . . .

The movies were thus a peerless school for building fantasy as fact, and the facts often survived one movie to live again in another, and another and others still to come. . . .

Lawrence Alloway remarks that the house of *The Magnificent Ambersons* (1942) shows up again in *The Fallen Sparrow* (1943), and Charles Higham points out that *Citizen Kane* (1941) contains clips from *The Hunchback of Notre Dame* (1939) and *Mary of Scotland* (1936), as well as a door left over from *Gunga Din* (1939) and some bats borrowed from *Son of Kong* (1933). *Julius Caesar* (1953), Bob Thomas suggests in his biography of Brando, was made so cheaply because it inherited a lot of scenery and costumes from *Quo Vadis?* (1951); and George N. Fenin and William K. Everson, in their book on westerns, remind us that *Geronimo* (1939) has footage from *The Plainsman* (1936), *Wells Fargo* (1937), and *The Thundering Herd* (1934); while *Laramie* (1950) uses all the big scenes from John Ford's *Stagecoach* (1939). I write in a later chapter of this book about Hollywood's well-known compulsion to repeat: not only were successful films remade all too frequently, they were often remade in disguise, with their plots transferred from India or the African desert to the American West; from Ireland to the American ghetto.

But even apart from such literal repetitions, the world of Hollywood movies clearly has a moral and physical geography of its own: a definite landscape. However little of it we have seen, we have seen a lot already. Wherever we came in, this is where we came in. "I thought they burned that," Groucho Marx says, looking at a child's sled called Rosebud. "Haven't we met someplace before?" Cary Grant asks Ralph Bellamy in *His Girl Friday* (1940). They have, three years before, in similar roles, in *The Awful Truth* (1937). Such allusions in Hollywood movies do not seem fussy or excessively self-conscious, as they would (and do) in novels, because they simply refer openly to what we all know: that the movies *are* a world, a country of familiar faces, a mythology made up of a limited number of stories.

Novels, with a few famous exceptions, usually pretend that we have never read a novel before in our lives, and may never read another after this one. Movies, on the other hand, tend to assume that we spend every waking moment at the pictures, that anyone who has found his or her way to the cinema is a moviegoer, a regular, an addict. "When I was twelve or thirteen," Fellini told Lillian Ross in an interview, "I went to movies all the time—American movies. But I did not know there were directors of movies. I always thought the actors did everything." We can't all sustain such innocence, any more than Fellini did, and we probably shouldn't try too hard. But Fellini's reminiscence confirms the sense of a world: we see movies as more or less continuous with each other. Movies rely on our experience of other movies, on a living tradition of the kind that literary critics always used to be mourning for, because it died in the seventeenth century or fizzled out with D. H. Lawrence. The movie tradition, of course, specializes in light comedy, well-made thrillers, frothy musicals, and weepy melodramas, rather than in such works as Donne's *Holy Sonnets* or George Eliot's *Middlemarch;* and we shouldn't listen too seriously to the siren voices of those critics who claim big things for Hollywood movies as art. But there *is* a tradition. We have in our heads as we sit in the cinema a sense of all the films we have seen, a range of common reference which is the Greek and Latin of the movies, our classical education. The classics here being the public's classics, rather than the critics': Fred Astaire rather than Flaherty; Lubitsch rather than von Stroheim.

The period I am concerned with in this book is roughly

the forties and the fifties, partly because the coherent world of the movies doesn't really assume its full and final form until about 1939 or a little earlier, and begins to dissolve again soon after 1960; and partly because those are the decades of my own innocent attendance at the movies, the time when I was a fully paid-up member of the universal movie audience—in the target area, as Lawrence Alloway says in his book *Violent America*. After that, like everyone else I knew, I became an inept but earnest student of film, and started trying to remember the names of directors. Then I worked as a writer on a couple of movies produced in England, and my innocence was really blown. Without knowing anything like enough, I already knew far too much.

But it is the sense of a world that really matters; and the sense of an age, of a heyday. The forties and fifties were an era of big stars, big studios, and big audiences—the weekly attendance at cinemas in America as late as 1951 was 90 million, falling to 43 million by the end of the decade. A lot of films and a lot of money were made during the thirties too, of course, but it was not really until the time of *Gone With The Wind* that Hollywood perfected that broad and knowing flamboyance which became its trademark. Thirties films tend to appear slightly too witty, too worldly, too remote by comparison. Think of Ronald Colman, and then think of Errol Flynn. Or think of Leslie Howard in *The Scarlet Pimpernel* (1933) and then again in *Gone With The Wind*. Think of Marlene Dietrich—Sternberg's Marlene Dietrich—and then think of Rita Hayworth. In each case, the second incarnation is brighter and richer, seems to call for a more immediate response from us; in each case, a certain amount of magic goes, a certain quantity of elegance and haze is exchanged for something clumsier.

There is one technical reason for some of this that is worth mentioning. Movies begin to look different because flat photography gives way to depth of focus, fast editing and figures filling the frame is replaced by composed frames, with groups of figures at varying distances from the camera. In the thirties we usually saw people against dim or blurred backgrounds. In the forties we saw *rooms*—perspectives. Since André Bazin's famous essay on the subject, depth of focus has been associated with *Citizen Kane*, but James Wong Howe, in an interview with Charles Higham, speaks of getting an illusion of depth as early as in *Transatlantic* (1931). Stanley Cortez, talking to Paul Mayersberg, said he and Arthur Miller and Gregg Toland (who shot *Citizen Kane*) were all working independently with deep focus at the same time, and added that they "made a transition from a romantic vision to a more realistic approach to the world." This is what matters. We begin to peer into a movie, rather than receive it in carefully arranged slices, with the camera flitting from speaker to speaker, and all feminine faces in soft focus. It is not exactly a question of realism, but it is a question of shedding romance and distance, of making the movie world more immediate and more accessible, more of a world.

Gone With The Wind, although not conspicuous for depth of focus, is the perfect instance of the new tone. Its passions are large and simple, it is full of wind-swept silhouettes caught against reddening skies. The grand moment of this unsubtle style—the spot where the broadness pays off—is of course the railway station at Atlanta. Vivien Leigh is looking for the doctor because Olivia de Havilland is about to give birth. We see her stepping gingerly over a wounded soldier or two, the camera moves backward and upward, we see more bodies lying there, and then more and more, till the whole screen fills with the sight of the technicolored sick and dying, the gallant, mangled South, while the sound track, with a touch of perfectly placed vulgarity, mingles "Tannenbaum" with a phrase from "Way Down Upon the Swanee River," and then imitates "The Last Post." Santa Maria, one might say.

At the end of the period we can, if we care to look, see it all coming apart in *Cleopatra*. The battle of Actium is a fiasco in a bathtub. Elizabeth Taylor, at the conclusion of a spectacular entry into Rome, winks cozily at Rex Harrison, in close-up. The two of them discuss Caesar's *Commentaries*. How do they compare with Catullus, Harrison slyly asks. Taylor says, "They're different." Richard Burton, as Antony, broods in a mausoleum and emerges to make a joke about his roommate—"or should I say tombmate?" He tries to commit suicide by driving his sword into his stomach and casually remarks, "I've always envied Ruffio his long arms." No doubt some of these jokes were inserted by Mankiewicz, the director, or improvised by the actors, to cheer themselves up during the ill-fated shooting of the film, but the point really is how those touches all fail to work. They fail because the movie fails generally, of course; but they also fail because their day is gone, because the time for overdoing things—jokes (Burton), vulgarity (Taylor), style and irony (Harrison)—is past. In 1956, in *The Ten Commandments*, Anne Baxter could say, "Moses, Moses, you splendid, stubborn, adorable fool," but by 1963, the year of *Cleopatra*, the reign of the perfectly overblown movie (to say nothing of the overblown epic) was finished.

I don't mean things changed overnight—at either end of the era—and I haven't been tidy or scholastic about dates. I have talked about thirties films and sixties films where they seemed to belong. I mean simply that I have mainly forties and fifties films in mind when I think of Hollywood movies.

It is time for a mild confession. This is another one of those books by foreigners about America: a book by an Englishman who lives in New York. It presents all the drawbacks of the foreigner's view, and I can only hope it shows a couple of the virtues. The great potential virtue, it seems to me, is a sight of things that have become invisible to the natives through familiarity or proximity, a sense of context and continuity where the natives tend to see only random change and crack-up. Not that the view is particularly cheerful. It is just that America remains American to me through all its shifts and switches and losses, where native Americans may feel it has become another place entirely, an unknown country.

I had originally intended to compare the America of the movies with the other America out there in reality and to pursue the comparison in some detail. But by the time I had finished my description of the first country, I seemed to have said quite a lot about the second already, and the relation between the two Americas seemed fairly clear: intricate, unstable, many-faced—but *clear*.

It is a relation of wish, echo, transposition, displacement, inversion, compensation, reinforcement, example, warning—there are virtually as many categories of the relation as you care to dream up, and I don't see why we should try to keep the number down. What remains constant is an oblique but unbroken connection to the historical world. All movies mirror reality in some way or other. There are no escapes, even in the most escapist pictures. In *Night and Day*, for example (1946)—a sloppy film biography of Cole Porter starring Cary Grant and aimed at soothing us all into a stupor—the Lusitania sinks, and Grant composes "Begin the Beguine" at the front, to the sound of falling bombshells and the "beat-beat-beat of the tom-toms" * (wrong song, but no matter) of a French African regiment.

The business of films is the business of dreams, as Nathanael West said, but then dreams are scrambled messages from waking life, and there is truth in lies, too, as Lamar Trotti wrote in the screenplay of *The Ox-Bow Incident* (1943), if you get enough of them. We are not likely to read too much into the usually rosy mirror-world of the movies, because we can't *not* see our world in the mirror. We do it all the time. We translate and interpret and transfer from films back to life, but we do it instantly and intuitively, working at a level of awareness somewhere just below full consciousness. Much of our experience of popular films—and of popular culture generally: jokes, plays, novels, songs, night-club acts, television shows and series—resides in the place we usually call the back of the mind, the place where we keep all those worries that won't come out into the open and won't go away either, that nag at us from the edges of consciousness. Movies bring out these worries without letting them loose and without forc-

* From the song "Night and Day" by Cole Porter. © 1932 Harms, Inc. Copyright Renewed. All Rights Reserved. Used by Permission of Warner Bros. Music.

ing us to look at them too closely. They trot around the park in the half-light and the exercise does us all good. Barbara Deming, in her fascinating (and sometimes irritating) *Running Away From Myself,* speaks of the "real magic" of the Hollywood film: "not only does it bring to the question the right answer; it brings the right answer without letting the audience become fully aware of what the question is." This is very perceptive, and I would add only that frequently there is not even a question, merely a hazy area of preoccupation, and that it doesn't appear to be necessary for a movie to solve anything, however fictitiously. It seems to be enough for us if a movie simply dramatizes our semi-secret concerns and contradictions in a story, allows them their brief, thinly disguised parade. Life goes on in the movie, scarcely shaken by the muffled incursion of our troubles, and the movie, by sympathetic magic, may induce life to go on outside it. What is the function of Sidney Poitier in a whole series of films, starting with *Edge of the City* (1957), if not to allude to our anxieties about race without really stirring them up? The allusion will not dispel our fears, but it will keep them quiet until we can get to see Poitier in another reassuring movie.

But movies are entertainment, aren't they? What is this talk of anxiety and sympathetic magic? They *are* entertainment, but the definition is not as comforting or as final as it looks. Why should we be entertained by *these* stories rather than by others? Why is pure escapism so difficult in movies? Why does the Lusitania keep sinking in films that really have no call for it? Or, to descend again on the unfortunate Poitier, whose dignity has somehow survived all those smiling, servile roles—even if it is true that Poitier is altogether too presentable, too much the black for people who don't like blacks—why bring up the question of race at all in the movies, if you just want to make money and keep people happy?

It seems that entertainment is not, as we often think, a full-scale flight from our problems, not a means of forgetting them completely, but rather a rearrangement of our problems into shapes which tame them, which disperse them to the margins of our attention. *For Me and My Gal* shows us a newspaper headline, dated 1916: GERMANS NEARING PARIS. But Gene Kelly, who is holding the paper, is not reading this. We are. He is looking for his name on another page. Later, another headline appears: LUSITANIA SUNK. But again, we are the ones who read this, because Kelly is asleep, with the newspaper covering his face. This seems to me almost a paradigm of the way entertainment so often works: The world of death and war and menace and disaster is really there, gets a mention, but then is rendered irrelevant by the story or the star or the music. The Lusitania sinks but Gene Kelly is asleep; the battle rages (in *Night and Day*) but Cary Grant is jotting down "Begin the Beguine."

"Leopards break into the temple," Kafka wrote, "and drink to the dregs what is in the sacrificial pitchers; this is repeated over and over again; finally it can be calculated in advance, and it becomes part of the ceremony." The parable describes many situations, both public and private, with uncomfortable precision. For the moment, though, we can see it as describing popular culture at work; and especially the movies. The leopards are all those alarms and preoccupations which we can't acknowledge and can't ignore, and the temple is the fiction which is supposed to entertain us. We can't do anything about the leopards breaking in, and still less can we do anything, it seems, about the actual existence of leopards in the world outside the temple. But while they are in the temple, we can surround them with a consoling or attenuating interpretation of their activity. They still drink the pitchers dry, and they are still, no doubt, dangerous. But they are no longer wild and meaningless; no longer stray, vicious animals haunting the borders of our mind. They are part of the ceremony.

All this makes the movies sound like the instrument of social prevention that many writers have seen in them: a means of keeping the discontented masses quiet, the new opium of the people. (David Robinson reflects a familiar view when he says, "The American studios . . . were dedicated to the manufacture of dreams to keep the nation content through stressful times.") Certainly the movies characteristically offer us packs of lies, but we would not consume these lies so avidly unless we needed them; thus, the target of our attack, if we are disposed to attack this state of affairs, should surely be the world which creates the need for such stories, rather than the stories themselves. There is something too conspiratorial and too literary about many Marxist views of popular culture— from those of Adorno and Horkheimer to those of Roland Barthes. The lies themselves are not the problem, and nothing will be gained by our unmasking them as lies if the world that made us need them remains unchanged. Demystification is an idle task if we still clamor for new mystifications at the end of it.

In any case, things are not often so drastic in the movies. No one is prevented from rushing to the barricades by seeing *Marty* (1955), not even by a lifetime of seeing films like *Marty*. What happens is that we don't worry about the leopards as often as we otherwise might—and there are all kinds of leopards anyway, large and small, major and minor. Movies preserve our moral slumber in the way that dreams are said to preserve our sleep, and only someone who stays awake twenty-four moral hours a day is in any real position to complain. Or to change the metaphor, movies are not our opium, they are only our placebo; our beer and skittles, and our pies in the sky. If they didn't exist, we would have to invent them.

The ceremony with the leopards comes very close to being a myth as myth has been defined by a number of recent writers, notably Lévi-Strauss—except that Lévi-Strauss, and before him Durkheim, insists rather too much on the infractions of logic that myths evoke and then palliate. "The purpose of myth," Lévi-Strauss writes, "is to provide a logical model capable of overcoming a contradiction"; and Lévi-Strauss quotes Durkheim as saying that totemic myths do not explain anything, but merely displace the difficulties they raise. In displacing them, however, they reduce their "logical scandal." I have myself talked quite a lot about logical contradictions in the pages that follow—about head-on conflicts between different but related American assumptions about experience—but this is really a matter of convenience. It sometimes clears things up a little to suggest that the leopards are warring assertions scattered about the country's moral and psychological life: Americans are generous (and that's good); Americans are energetically selfish (and that's good too); women are born guilty, but women are eternally pure; success makes you lonely and nasty, but we all want success; we have to believe our eyes, but we can't believe our eyes. But my general feeling is that films deal mainly in worries that are not so much contradictory as muddled, clumsily overlapping, unexamined. The mythological function of the movies is to examine them without seeming to look at them at all. Movies assuage the discomforts of blurred minds; but they also maintain the blur. That is their business.

"Problems (or less directly, the preoccupations they cause)," G. S. Kirk writes in his study of myth, "are reflected in mythical narratives," and at times the

mere reflexion or expression [of the problems] seems to serve as an outlet or incentive for the makers of myth, without doing much more, and touches a response in successive audiences. More frequently the myth offers an apparent way out of the problem, either by simply obfuscating it, or making it appear abstract and unreal. . . .

This seems to me wonderfully exact, although I must add, for my purposes here, that coherent and complete myths are not as frequent in movies as they sometimes seem. What are frequent are fragments of myth, mythological snatches at parts of a problem, hints at large, encompassing myths that rarely seem to materialize themselves. I began this book with the idea of using myths to map the world of Hollywood movies, but I found the myths were mostly too fragmented or too scattered to be the right tools for this job. The ensuing chapters focus, therefore, on the clusters of worries, on the areas of concern which employ myths for their expression, rather than on the myths themselves. I have written a good deal about myths, but they are ceremonies, and I have come to be more preoccupied with the leopards. My investigation, of course, is far from exhaustive. There are plenty more leopards where these came from. And I should perhaps add, in view of those ominous scholarly names I have just introduced, that I am not using the word myth, when I do use it, in any special way. Movies seem to me to offer myths (or pieces of myths) in just the way in which a unicorn is seen as a mythological beast: It doesn't exist, but it bears a striking and interesting resemblance to a horse.

One last introductory remark. The way Hollywood movies are made is so complicated, the result of so many different pressures and commitments and speculations and deals, that it is sometimes hard to see how these films can mean anything at all, let alone articulate the kind of buried worries I have excavated in this book. Anyone who has read Leo Rosten's *Hollywood*, or Lillian Ross's *Picture*, or Philip French's *The Movie Moguls*, knows something of what goes on behind the studio scenes, and even if you have never read a book about the movies in your life, you probably still can recall a few anecdotes about how a film was made simply because a star had to work off a contract; how a totally improbable and unsuitable part was written into a film so that a particular actor or actress could play in it; how studio bosses inflicted their own (usually garish) tastes on all the movies in their hands; how films were shot too fast, and edited into something quite different from what the director intended; how a director rarely used to get a chance to edit his own film; how so many movies were conceived and executed as mere hack work, jobs that had to be done; how so many movies were cooked up according to weary old recipes that once upon a time had spelled success. There is all this, and more. One is tempted to believe that the movies can be seen only as the end product of a series of cancellations and compromises, as the expression of nothing but the complicated history of their arrival on the screen.

Yet the myths and the worries are there, clearly inscribed in the movies themselves; and the reason is not hard to find. Hollywood is an industry, but it is an industry of guesses, and how can guesses at what people want *not* be mythological? Moviemakers are like sailors, as Margaret Thorp said long ago, forever wondering what the sea is going to do next. And wondering about it a year or so in advance too. It is a highly speculative, unpredictable game. If the public seems extraordinarily malleable at times, a population of suckers for any old rubbish, it can also be extraordinarily resistant both to rubbish and to masterpieces, when they fail to strike the right chord. It is worth recalling, if only in schematic, caricatured form, the essential structure of the industry in its great days: settled financiers on the East Coast were investing in uprooted adventurers on the West Coast because of their supposed expertise on the subject of what the Middle West really wanted. The movies did not describe or explore America, they invented it, dreamed up an America all their own, and persuaded us to share the dream. We shared it happily, because the dream was true in its fashion—true to a variety of American desires—and because there weren't all that many other dreams around. But given this unreality at the heart of the business, we should perhaps reverse our questions and our doubts, and ask, not how so many interesting meanings crept into flawed and ephemeral films, but how these films could possibly have kept such meanings out. Even trivial lies are a form of confession; even thin and calculated dreams have secrets to give away.

II

America First

HUMPHREY BOGART sits at a table behind a drink, moodily staring into the middle distance, a glint of heroic self-pity in his eyes. We are looking at a shot from *Casablanca* (1943) which has come to represent for many people the essence not only of that film but of Bogart's whole screen personality. Blown up into a poster, and scattered through the clubs, cafés, foyers, flats, dens, and dormitories of the Western world, it offers a maudlin echo to an equally famous poster of Ché Guevara: the mask of romantic introspection answers the mask of romantic action.

There is a great deal of anachronism in the confrontation, of course. For the Bogart of the poster is not the forties Bogart; he is merely a sixties dropout who has borrowed his face. Yet across the anachronism a certain quality remains, an aspect of the shot both then and now. For, whatever else it may have been or become, the shot is a portrait of a mood that goes well beyond *Casablanca* and beyond Bogart. It is a picture of what isolation looks like at its best: proud, bitter, mournful, and tremendously attractive. The sadness in the picture and the faint moral censure the film tempts us to apply ("You want to feel sorry for yourself, don't you?" Ingrid Bergman asks Bogart. "With so much at stake all you can think of is your own feeling") merely help us on our way to reveling in that consummate, paradoxical loneliness, the goal of so many unconfessed or half-confessed longings. We long to be lonely, that is, even as we go in search of others, and *Casablanca* plays out this puzzle perfectly. (By *we* I mean everyone who feels this way, although Americans, it seems to me, are the true authors and owners of this feeling. The rest of the world just clutches at it now and then.) Bogart gets Bergman back ("We'll always have Paris," they say), then gives her away again. They have all the glory of a great love, but they don't have to go on living with it, and Bogart strolls off to the war with Claude Rains, for all the world like Huck Finn lighting out for the Territory, or a cowboy riding thoughtfully out of the frame when all the feudin's done.

Of course, things are a little more complicated than that, but I'm not trying to simplify the picture. On the contrary, I'm trying to show how much there is in it. To be precise, then, Bogart gives up Bergman for a cause greater than his love. "Where I'm going you can't follow," he tells her. "What I've got to do, you can't be any part of.

Ilsa, I'm no good at being noble, but it doesn't take much to see that the problems of three little people don't amount to a hill of beans in this crazy world. Someday you'll understand that." As a matter of fact, she understands it already, since she said much the same thing to Bogart himself a couple of reels back, and it's not really clear why she can be a part of Paul Henreid's mission and not of Bogart's. Or rather, it is clear that what matters here, as in so much sentimental fiction, is that the lovers should be separated, however briskly or blandly the separation is effected. Bergman is returned to her husband, and Bogart is returned to his loneliness. Of course, he is going off with Claude Rains, forsaking a woman and peacetime for war and male comradeship, and I shall come back to this subject. Indeed, he is off to a war that American isolationists tried to keep their country out of, but this is just where the movie fades away. We don't see the war film that Bogart and Rains go off to star in, and what remains of *Casablanca* when it's over is not really those two setting off arm in arm for combat and adventure, and not Bogart and Bergman in Paris ("Was that cannon fire," Bergman asks, "or is it my heart pounding?" Bogart, ever the tough guy, says, "Ah, that's the new German 77"). What remains is the earlier Bogart who survived into the poster, alone, bitter, private, immersed in grief, cut off from the whole of humanity, miserable but *free*.

There are a number of sarcastic allusions to isolationism in the screenplay. "I stick my neck out for nobody," Bogart says more than once; Rains tells him that that is a "wise foreign policy," and later remarks that Bogart is "completely neutral about everything." The vast and sinister Sidney Greenstreet asks Bogart when he will realize that "in this world today isolationism is no longer a practical policy."

These are, I take it, merely topical sarcasms aimed, once the war is on, at all those who thought America could stay out of it. Or perhaps the suggestion is simply that America, like Bogart, is not really isolationist at heart, just reluctant to interfere in the affairs of others, and a little prone to hide its passionate altruism behind a mask of selfishness and diffidence ("Ilsa, I'm no good at being noble"). The corollary would be that when America does interfere, it completely runs the show and wins the war. Conrad Veidt, as the German commander, sees in Bogart "just another blundering American," but Rains tells him he mustn't underestimate American blundering, because he was with them when they "blundered" into Berlin in 1918.

In fact, all this gets lost in the movie, or rather is simply taken over by Bogart as the luminously lonely hero. An attempt to give a mild political edge to what is really a romantic, personal predicament (Bogart used to be a bit of a crusader before Bergman left him in Paris; in fact, he was the reverse of an isolationist, having fought in Spain and Abyssinia) turns out to lend Bogart's personal authority to a diffuse and fading political movement. I mean, I think, that the charms of isolation can be seen to outlive the vagaries and even the death of isolationism—that, in the end, they really don't have too much to do with isolationism at all—and these charms are the elusive subject of this chapter.

The subject is so vast and scattered and changing that I have been sorely tempted to leave it alone altogether. But it crops up in too many American movies, in its various disguises, and lies across the path of too many discussions of America. It is what we might call simply isolationism if the term didn't seem to restrict us to foreign policy, and if the historical phenomenon of that name were not made up of so many eccentric and unmanageable components; what we might call individualism if the word had not become so much of a slogan, and if anyone knew what it meant; what we might call selfishness if the concept didn't belong to a vocabulary of moral disapproval quite alien to the subject we are concerned with; what we might call loneliness if loneliness didn't seem so accidental a condition, so little the result of an energetic, almost ideological, choice. We could say the subject is selfishness when it covers personal relations, individualism when it covers the relation of the private person to society, and isolationism when it covers the relation of America to the rest of the world, but that is altogether too neat, and implies equations across the board that I don't like and don't need.

I want to suggest that there is in America a dream of freedom which appears in many places and many forms, which lies somewhere at the back of several varieties of isolationism and behind whatever we mean by individualism, which converts selfishness from something of a vice into something of a virtue, and which confers a peculiar, gleaming prestige on loneliness. It is a dream of freedom from others; it is a fear, to use a sanctioned and favorite word, of entanglement. It is what we mean when we say, in our familiar phrase, that we don't want to get involved.

Another portrait of Bogart helps to clarify some of this—not a poster this time, but the words of Alistair Cooke. Cooke, in *A Generation on Trial* (1950), identified a fast-ripening American breed of the unfooled, the chronically unconvinced, the man who before the appeal of conflicting certainties keeps up a hardboiled neutrality. This mode of feeling, developed as a mask by the generation that hurt its ideals in the First World War, has already passed into American literature and journalism as a narrative style in novels and news magazines. In the movies it has thrown up one favourite contemporary type—the "private eye" as played by Humphrey Bogart. In life it provides a useful refuge in skepticism for people who don't propose to sacrifice comfort to principle; for it is surely a disguised form of playing safe and the easiest parody of serenity available to the bewildered and the thoroughly scared.

This is a very fine perception, and it is true that Cooke is thinking not of the Bogart of *Casablanca*, but of Bogart's Sam Spade in *The Maltese Falcon* (1941) and his Philip Marlowe in *The Big Sleep* (1946)—a weary private eye is not the same thing as a hurt lover. Nevertheless, Cooke has subtly borrowed Bogart for his own purposes. He is writing about the case of Hiss and Chambers, and there was a question of genuine choice and genuine neutrality there, of course. You decided one of these men was telling the truth, or you decided not to decide. Yet the Bogart figure in the movies is never really faced with "conflicting certainties." He is never really in any doubt as to which side he will join if he joins the battle. He is not trying to decide who is right, or refusing to decide who is right. He knows who is right, just as America knew that if it intervened in World War II, it would be on the side of the Allies. And this is the point. A consistent thread in traditional isolationism, perfectly echoed in Bogart and other lonely heroes, is a worry, not about your enemies, whom you face with reckless daring, but about your friends, and the demands they will make on you after the war, the contamination of an essential liberty which they will represent. You hesitate, not about combat and not about which army to support, but about the strings to be tied around your neck. " 'Tis our true policy to steer clear of permanent alliances," Washington said; and Jefferson's phrase was "peace, commerce, and honest friendship with all nations, entangling alliances with none." The principle, it seems to me, reaches into many areas of American life. Society itself, marriage, requited love, and (in the movies) most strongly felt relationships except all-male camaraderie: all are versions of the entangling alliance. A man has to move on; and there is a fear and a superstitition at work here which is nowhere to be found in Washington or Jefferson. It is the fear that all alliances are entangling alliances. Conversely, putting ourselves first (or putting America first: the America First Committee was a leading isolationist organization, formed in 1940) seems to be a way of staving off those encircling and encroaching on *others*. The self will save us from our friends.

In reality, of course, we all make marriages and alliances, live in society, tie ourselves to others in all kinds of ways. But then reality can be remarkably unsatisfactory, and I am interested in what we think we give up when we enter those entangling relations. Europeans, for example, are *born* entangled, and harbor only the most diffident and complicated dreams of escape from others. Americans, on the other hand, are the children of Rousseau to a greater extent than we shall ever chart, and they start from isolation as a primary or desired condition. This doesn't make Americans isolationists, since most are ready to trade in their isolation when the time seems right to them. But it does tinge all their relations with others—other nations, other people—with a shade of reluctance. From Wilson's speech about joining the European war in 1917 (he advised Congress "that it formally accept the status of belligerent which has thus been thrust upon it") to Nixon's edgy remarks in 1974 about a "new spirit of isolationism" growing in America, passing through countless individual and domestic instances we can all think of, there is the same unhappiness, the same sense of punctured privacy, of glum acceptance of the consequences of living in an inhabited world. It is not really a question of the geographical isolation of America, ended now in any case by jet travel, long-distance missiles, and an unfortunate imperial destiny. Nor is it a question of America's having been founded, and regularly renewed, by a flight from old Europe. It is not even a question of legends of self-help and myths of the frontier, nor of the sanctity of the individual. Or rather it is a question of all that, and much more, brewing at the back of American minds, rankling as a mild (and sometimes not so mild) resentment against the need for others which the modern world insists on, which Europeans accept as a perennial fact of life, and which Americans see as a version of the Fall, the lapse of Rousseau's natural man into the compromise and frustration of social life as we know it.

The Fall has no dates, of course, and is not marked on any calendar. It is the moment at which American individuals lose their innocence; when their existence, in Henry James's wonderful phrase, becomes complicated by a regret; when they find that the social contract, their entanglement with others, costs them more than they are really willing to pay. But it is a moment in myth, not in time. James placed it in the Civil War. Many people (myself included) have located it in the American engagement in Vietnam. In fact, the Fall will take place as often as Americans worry about their relation to society and the world, and for as long as they believe that the individual, the human creature left entirely to his own devices, has some sort of inherent innocence to lose. Once that belief goes, there is nothing to be lost, no Adam left to fall; until then the myth will borrow whatever historical material it needs, from Shiloh to My Lai, and on to the conquest of Mars. Because American innocence has no historical home, it can dwell where it likes in history.

The resentment against others often takes exaggerated, almost diagrammatic forms in American films, as in those numerous movies which assert the absolute right of the hero not to lift a finger to help anyone if he doesn't feel like it. Once this right is clearly seen and agreed on (by the audience, that is, since there are always one or two softies in these films—usually women and old men—who exhibit kindlier sentiments), the hero can go into action and literally wallow in altruistic good deeds. In *China* (1943), for example, Alan Ladd on the road to Shanghai knocks down his friend William Bendix rather than agree with Loretta Young and turn back in order to save a few lives. Business and self-assertion first. Having knocked Bendix down, Ladd confesses that he was going to turn back anyway. The "faithless gesture," as Barbara Deming says, "is given expression, and then denied." Except that it is not a faithless gesture at all, but the expression of a faith, of a dogged belief in the primacy of one's debts to oneself over all other debts, and the denial of the gesture fools no one. Ladd has established selfishness as a fierce moral ideal in its own right, and the conventional ethic to which he then surrenders is tame by comparison. We see this story acted out again and again in American life, as millionaires (or corporations) first make their fortunes, *and then* start spreading benefactions all over the place.

Another schematic form of the resentment against others is the fable that sees individualism as sheer flamboyant stubbornness. In *The Sheepman* (1958), Glenn Ford tries to graze sheep near a cattle town. After a number of tricks and trials, he finally forces the town to accept his sheep, much against its will, and at the price of several dramatic shoot-outs and showdowns. Then he sells his sheep, and buys cattle. This last touch, along with one or two other moments in the film, converts a movie about tolerance and democracy, about the rights of all kinds of people to farm the open spaces of America, sheepmen as well as cattlemen, into a plea for rampant, quirky orneriness, for the right of the individual to do exactly as he pleases. With the corollary, to be sure, that he has to carve out this right for himself; thus, Ford's first serious action in town is to beat up the local tough guy, just to let people know he is not to be crowded. "Nobody's going to tell me what to do," he says. "I guess I'm just stubborn."

Selfishness as an ideal, individualism as stubbornness. These are simple, trivial expressions of the resentment against others, as insecure as they are shallow and aggressive. For a sense of the complexity and ubiquity and authentic appeal of the American myth of a Fall into social life, we need to look at some of its more oblique and intricate manifestations: selfishness elevated into a source of energy, identified with life itself; a concern for particular people seen as the only recourse against inhuman abstraction; individualism cast as a discreet, all-encompassing nostalgia for an earlier stage of American society.

Gone With The Wind is an interesting instance, because

both Margaret Mitchell's book and the movie are haunted by the ghosts of half a dozen nineteenth-century European novels, *Wuthering Heights* and *Vanity Fair* prominent among them, and the ghosts have been curiously changed by the Atlantic crossing. Selfishness in European novels is often attractive but it is always morally shady. Selfishness in America is so attractive that it is always threatening to get out of hand, and no sort of censure really touches it. Margaret Mitchell neatly masks the problem by setting a romance of failure, the gallant South incarnate in Leslie Howard and Olivia de Havilland, against the unscrupulous, tenacious lives of Vivien Leigh and Clark Gable. A fading breed of nice people, patently unfit to survive in a rough world, thus cloaks and legitimizes the ruthlessness of those who do survive. If selfishness is what it takes to keep going, who can be against it?

Two small examples. When Vivien Leigh, still in mourning for her young husband, dances with Clark Gable at the charity bazaar, the splash of her black gown among the light-colored suits and dresses of the other dancers is both scandalous and exciting, a sort of metaphor for the rights of the lively self against all its composed and respectable enemies—except that normal associations are here reversed, and black becomes the badge of a striking individual life, while other colors are merely the uniform of an insipid society. Selznick was speaking of a later part of *Gone With The Wind* when he said that it should, "by its colors alone, dramatize the difference between Scarlett and the rest of the people," but that is precisely what happens at the ball. (Selznick also spoke of taking the opportunity to "throw a violent dab of color at the audience to sharply make a dramatic point.")

Later in the movie, Vivien Leigh is nursing the

wounded of the Civil War, then gives up and goes home, because she can't stand it any more. In a European novel, and probably in a European movie, we would understand how she felt but not expect her to give in to her feelings. In *Gone With The Wind*, we may feel vaguely disapproving, may feel she ought to have stayed, but essentially we are with her, I think. If she's had enough, she's had enough, and with all those maimed soldiers lying about one nurse more or less is not going to make any difference. We concur, that is, when Leigh gets tired of altruism, and everything in the film is geared to making us concur. I don't mean to suggest that this was Selznick's conscious plan, or even Margaret Mitchell's, merely that this was the way it turned out. *Gone With The Wind*, whatever its other virtues and failings, and whatever its intentions, is one of the great American celebrations of self.

I should insist that such celebrations are not rebellions of the self against society, for the simple reason that society, in the sense of the dense, dead medium in which European lives are embroiled, doesn't exist in America. It is not just that the Americans don't have Ascot, as Henry James said; they don't even have Coronation Street. Society exists in America in the way that towns exist in westerns: If you step through one of those false fronts you're in the desert or in the studio, off into the wilderness or off into make-believe. American fictions, that is, do not condone selfishness, and their official moral language, as it were, is that of any European country: responsibility, duty to society, debts to others, and so on. It is just that the energies of these fictions lie elsewhere. Bogart, Gable, Ladd (and later William Holden and Robert Mitchum)— what these actors represent, in numerous movies, is not only a certain heroism of self, but a very slender grasp of the arguments *against* selfishness, especially slender in the case of social arguments, which tend to crumble in the face of such charisma. Americans, one might say, are vulnerable to glamorous pleas for the self in the way the French are vulnerable to invocations of logic, or the English to appeals to fair play.

Another American film haunted by old-world ghosts is Hathaway's *Lives of a Bengal Lancer* (1935). The setting of Empire in India, like the echoes of European novels in *Gone With The Wind*, reinforces rather than reduces the Americanness of the movie's major concerns. Richard Cromwell, as the son of the commanding officer of one of Britain's brave outposts, falls for a beautiful spy, and is whisked away to the hideout of the local Afghan enemy. The boy's father, determined not to show any favoritism, will not take his regiment to rescue him because his duty is to the Queen Empress and his men, not to his defecting son. Gary Cooper and Franchot Tone decide that this talk of duty is entirely inhuman, and take off to rescue the boy—they desert, that is, from the army of abstraction in the name of an individual case. But having asserted humanity against duty, the film now must affirm some forms of duty against sheer self-indulgence—can't have every soldier deserting when he feels the army's not human enough for him. This is brilliantly done by having Cromwell crack under torture, while Cooper and Tone, also captured by the evil Afghan, take their medicine like heroes, suffer horribly for the sake of the duty they have just abandoned, because they won't betray their regiment to the enemy. Cooper indeed, talking to Cromwell, literally echoes a lecture we have heard earlier in the film, about the white man's burden and the handful of heroic, unsung fellows who hold a whole troublesome continent.

He evokes as his creed, that is, the code he has just re-
volted against, and dies in a subsequent skirmish, killed
off, we may feel, by the contradiction he stumbled into.
(Eighteen years later, in *From Here to Eternity* (1953),
Montgomery Clift represented the stubborn, noble self
against the heavy hand of the American army, but the
central issue was once again elegantly fudged: this was a
peacetime army, and when Pearl Harbor came, Clift tried
to get back to do his duty. The army had not been asking
Clift to do his real duty but a phony duty, in the form of
boxing for the regiment when he didn't want to; and like
Cooper, he was killed anyway, a victim of the awkward
questions his character and presence seemed to raise.)

Of course there is no direct question of selfishness in
Lives of a Bengal Lancer. Cooper's contradiction reflects two
sets of *others*, the whole army and one friend. I want to
suggest, though, that Cooper's revolt against duty in the
name of humanity is completely convincing, because it appeals to a sense of an individual human self, while his mar-
tyr's death for queen and country seems exotic and unlikely, an instance of that old masochistic British
eccentricity (Cooper is supposed to be Canadian, which
makes the gesture all the more quixotic). There is a form
of pragmatism in operation here, which insists on the particular person as someone we can *know*, and therefore feel
something for, while an abstraction like duty remains
only an abstraction. Cooper again, in *Return to Paradise*
(1953), is invited to help the natives of a Pacific island to
rid themselves of a tyrant. He won't, because it's every
man for himself in this life, he says. His dad was a be-
liever in causes and got himself killed for his belief. Then
the tyrant starts to tyrannize a girl, and Cooper deals with
him. This pattern occurs again and again in American

37

movies, especially since Pearl Harbor. A hero who will
not sign up for a cause (because he only believes in people
and because, like Bogart in *Casablanca*, he's no good at
being noble) joins the fray when a person he cares about
(almost always a girl) is hurt or threatened. He joins the
fray on the right side, of course: against the Germans or
the Japanese if it's World War II, against the Chinese if
they're against the missionaries, against Maximilian in
Mexico, and so on. There is a clear suggestion that we had
nothing ideological against Hitler, we just didn't like the
way he pushed people around (Gary Cooper himself,
questioned by the House Un-American Activities Committee, said he didn't know much about communism, but
as far as he could tell, he was against it, because it didn't
seem to him to be "on the level").

Assertions of self find a useful ally in pragmatism. They
find an even more useful one in psychoanalysis, which is
easily cast as a doctrine of self-help. Neither Marx nor
Jesus, Jean-François Revel said of America. Not Marx but
Freud, one might add. Not sociology but psychology; not
society's ills but yours and mine. Even movies that tacitly
admit that the country is going through a bad spell, like
The Best Years of Our Lives (1946), still contrive to suggest
that the fault lies with the individual who can't pull himself together. Thus, there are no jobs for you, and this
might seem to be a fact about society rather than your
psyche. Then you pull yourself together, like Dana Andrews in this movie, and magically a job appears. There *is*
no social world out there, there is only a system of rewards for self-confidence and of penalties for losing faith.

Of course, a great deal of American toughness is merely
the gruff voice in which true kindness speaks. Or rather
both toughness and kindness coexist in the same desire: a

desire to be enormously generous and narrowly selfish at one and the same time. A major function of all the movies I am discussing here is to bring this contradiction out into the daylight, or at least the twilight. We can see it now; it's not skulking at the edge of our vision, irritating us like a speck on a mirror. Yet we can't see it too clearly; we are not hurt by the violence of the contradiction. Barbara Deming illustrates all this beautifully at the start of *Running Away From Myself*: Eisenhower explains that America's interest in Vietnam is an investment in Southeast Asia, a good business deal; and then he explains it as the selfless support of a people fighting for its freedom. There is no reason why both these explanations should not be true, on some level of double-think and self-deception, and one can see why, practically, an American president might have to offer first one explanation then another. But in the context I am trying to create, the contradiction is not accidental, not the result of day-to-day political expediencies. It is at the heart of an American puzzle about our relations with others, for both generosity and selfishness are unilateralist, isolationist attitudes, depending only on our will and our condescension, on our acceptance or refusal of community. We are benign or indifferent gods, ready to do business with humanity only on our terms, and I need to turn now from the attractions of the self to the self's social policies, to that large rejection of the whole of modern civil life that is so persistently enacted in American movies.

Barbara Deming extracts a nice progression from some films of the forties. That favorite figure, the disabled hero (John Garfield, say, in *Pride of the Marines*, 1945), comes to stand for all returning soldiers, disabled or not, unsure that there is really a place for them in civilian society. (*The Best Years of Our Lives*, although not mentioned by Deming, is the perfect example.) But then these returning soldiers themselves represent many American men, in and out of war, men who are not sure that society offers a home to them, men for whom society is rather a trap and a prison, contrasted with the freedom of the skies (*Those Endearing Young Charms*, 1945) or the vastness of the ocean (*Adventure*, 1945). These heroes, according to Deming, are people who question "not simply the possibilities of a particular marriage but the possibilities of any sort of life 'on land,' any sort of life within existing society." *Existing society* is rather too hopeful a phrase: What these men question is the possibility of any sort of life within any sort of society, and the extremity of this position accounts for the faint currents of despair and panic that run beneath the bland surfaces of these fairly forgettable films.

The girl in all these situations, as Miss Deming suggests, is Ariadne, winding the man back out of the labyrinth of his loneliness and into ordinary domestic life, and there is an eerie, animal echo of the theme in Disney's *The Lady and the Tramp* (1955), where the Tramp, who is nobody's dog and has never worn a collar, who is a great lover and Don Juan along the lines of Douglas Fairbanks, Jr., ends up collared and married, husband of the Lady, and proud, submissive father of a fine batch of pups.

The hero is drawn, Deming notes, into a life he refuses to believe in for himself, into the heroine's arms, where "life begins." Just so. Except that "life begins" is pure assertion, like Bogart's contribution to the war effort in *Casablanca*, since the movies end just there. Home is what we know we ought to want but can't really take. America is

Pride of the Marines (1945): The end of independence—a blind John Garfield, trying to get along without Eleanor Parker, knocks over a Christmas tree and starts his readjustment to civilian life. Copyright © 1945 Warner Bros. Pictures, Inc. Renewed 1972.

not so much a home for anyone as a universal dream of home, a wish whose attraction depends upon its remaining at the level of a wish. The movies bring the boys back but stop as soon as they get them back; for home, that vaunted, all-American ideal, is a sort of death, and an oblique justification for all the wandering that kept you away from it for so long.

"When the man (in the movies) goes home to his wife," Stanley Cavell writes in *The World Viewed*, "his life is over." "In a thousand other instances," Cavell continues, "the marriage must not be seen, and the walk into the sunset is into a dying star: they live happily ever after—as long as they keep walking." Rhetorical exaggeration apart, this is a remarkable insight, as is Cavell's next comment: that the only believable families in American films appear in the setting of an elegiac past, because movies characteristically assert community not through the family but through male comradeship. "The military man," Cavell says, "asserts the myth of community, the idea that society is man's natural state," and women and children break or end these idylls.

A remarkable insight, as I say, an exact perception of the normal relation between men and women in American movies. But the perception is also exactly upside down. It is women who assert the myth of community in the movies, who propose a world of children and homes and porches and kitchens and neighbors and gossip and schools—everything the American hero is on the run from; and it is men in groups who represent a temporary, wishful exemption from this grim destiny. That is, community is scarcely asserted at all in American movies, except sentimentally and rhetorically, and I don't think there is anyone in America who believes that society is "man's natural state." Community is simply replaced by corporate masculine adventures, of which war is the most common and most easily available. When community is asserted, it is asserted by women, as a form of entanglement, a dark snare almost always eclipsed by the glamour of loneliness and wandering.

Of male loneliness and wandering, to be sure; and all this says a great deal about the relations between the sexes in America—or at least about the way we choose (or used to choose) to see the relations between the sexes. But that is for another chapter. For the moment I wish just to say again that women in the movies are the privileged representatives of society and civilized life, that marriage is the emblem of many entangling alliances, and that Philip French's remarks, which follow, do not apply only to westerns, which are French's subject:

the hero secretly fears women and the civilization, compromise and settled life they represent; he sees them as sources of corruption and betrayal, luring him away from independence and a sure sense of himself as well as from the more comforting company of men.

In Anthony Mann's *The Far Country* (1955), Corinne Calvet invokes the loneliness of an old man as an argument in favor of marriage and gregariousness. James Stewart dourly replies, "Maybe he likes to be lonely, ever think of that?"

Thus, we are back at *Casablanca*, with Bogart staring into his drink or going off with Claude Rains; or, to stay in the West, we are in John Sturges's *The Law and Jake Wade* (1958), where deciding to get married simply ruins Robert Taylor as a cowboy, and even the camera, for the whole last section of the film, takes the bad guy's part, follows him around, endorses, literally, his point of view, so that Taylor becomes the virtuous heavy, the victorious pillar of society, and Richard Widmark, as the bad guy, dies the death of the romantic outlaw, hounded by the narrow, civilized justice of the modern world.

It is time, perhaps, to talk more directly of westerns. The shoot-out between Taylor and Widmark in *The Law and Jake Wade* is itself a version of America's Fall into society, of course. Widmark dies, and Taylor abandons the only form of life that matters to us in westerns, the lonely, unsettled, embattled career of the outlaw, the sheriff, or the range-hand; roles and jobs which guarantee movement, peril, and a radical separation from one's fellow men. Westerns occasionally show us a bit of male comradeship at the bunkhouse, but usually even this limited, all-male community is too much for the hero, who ends up riding on, headed for the next town or the next state in an infinite America. But the hero doesn't ride on before he's done his job, and westerns are by no means unequivocal hymns to the individual. The lonely wanderer frequently helps to found a society he himself can have no part of, and there is a genuine pathos here. Where the broken but untamed modern characters picked up by the American Ariadne had to be reclaimed for the contemporary world, the Westerner is already lost to that world, member of an old order we all know has gone. Nostalgia has riddled westerns since Fenimore Cooper, and titles like *The Last Roundup* (1934), *The Last of the Comanches* (1952), *The Last Frontier* (1956), and *The Last Wagon* (1956) are all too common. It is true that Hollywood is fond of the elegiac mode generally, but westerns are elegiac by definition.

What is interesting is that this nostalgia is built not on a rejection of the modern world but on a sad acceptance of

The Law and Jake Wade (1958): Civilization and Its Malcontents—
Robert Taylor, Richard Widmark, and the Rockies enact the fall
of America. From the MGM release *The Law and Jake Wade*. ©
1958 Loew's, Incorporated.

it. The price of civilization is seen to be cruelly high, but westerns don't refuse to pay it. They pause at the moment of payment, invite us to contemplate the cost even as they trade in their adventure and isolation for a placid safety in numbers. They represent not a denial of the social contract but a desire to return to the time before its consequences began to make themselves so drastically felt, to a time before things turned out the way they did. The law is established in the West, or the marshal arrives, and the bad guys depart and die. Yet the movie itself shows us one last desperate fight to hold the town jail, or drive a tyrant out of town—just the sort of heroic exploit that the arrival of the law will make unnecessary, even impossible.

There is a fine ambivalence here because of the way Americans worship the law as something beyond politics, almost beyond human fallibility. "The law," Dana Andrews writes before he dies in *The Ox-Bow Incident*, "is what everybody's ever thought about justice, about right and wrong. It's the conscience of humanity." And Henry Fonda as the young Mr. Lincoln, in John Ford's movie of that title (1939), muses on Blackstone's *Commentaries* and thinks, "By Gee, that's all there is to it. Right and wrong." (Admittedly, Lamar Trotti wrote the screenplay for both of those movies, so the law there may be a personal hobbyhorse rather than an American idol.) Louis Hartz, in *The Liberal Tradition in America*, speculates on the "unusual power of the Supreme Court, and the cult of constitution worship on which it rests," and remarks that in England, say, it would be unthinkable that "the largest issues of public policy should be put before nine Talmudic judges examining a single text." What this means in westerns is that the law is a real answer to the single self that goes so unchecked in other movies. The arrival of the law, so often the subject of westerns, can't be regretted or diminished or discarded, scuttled by the charisma of a hero's egoism. (Gangster movies are different, because they are about law *enforcement* which doesn't draw on the same pieties.) But even with all this, an ambivalence remains. The law brings civilization with it, or rather the law and civilization at this stage are the same thing, with the banks and the railroad and the telegraph as incidental, irritating features, the forerunners of big capitalism. Thus the law, which can do no wrong, brings trouble and corruption in its wake. The law is the serpent that sets up the Fall, and Fenin and Everson in their book on westerns point out the interesting frequency of crimes that use the law in these movies, of crimes that are in fact legal. The villains know the newly arrived laws by heart and apply them to chiseling simple folks out of their land and their stock, and they often have the sheriff in their pocket.

The Spoilers, a western set in the north and so popular a story that it was remade every decade from 1914 until the fifties, explores a good deal of this ambivalence about the Law. I am thinking of the 1942 version. A man asks if there is a room in a boarding house and is turned away because the place is full. Shots are heard, and a body tumbles downstairs. Just a minute, the manager says, we have a room, one of our guests just checked out. Lawlessness is the subject of a casual wisecrack, and it is clearly preferable to the smooth legal evil of the rotten judge and Randolph Scott, the citified man behind him. The arrival of the law is merely the arrival of a new form of criminality, and only our hero, John Wayne, can resolve these contradictions and preserve the community from both its initial anarchy and its present injustice under the law. But then the hero introduces a new contradiction, and one which dogs many westerns: How can a justice which is founded on the heroic action of an individual become the justice of an invariably cowardly group of townsfolk or settlers? Westerns regularly end on this question, which leaves us with society seemingly ordered, but owing everything to the lonely character it now has no room for. Sometimes this state of affairs is rubbed in by a sermon, ideally delivered by James Stewart: democracy is praised, isolated deeds of valor played down. But then the movie itself, apart from such speeches, tilts entirely the other way.

Think of what westerns look like. That dusty street, those creaking sidewalks, the saloon, the bank, sometimes a newspaper office. It is the same scene in virtually every western, almost enough to establish a genre in its own right, without any people in it; the same ramshackle, just-begun town. Whatever its supposed location in a given movie, it is an image of the frontier, of society starting in the wilderness, and its echo and counterpart is the ghost town. "Fastest growing town in the territory," a sign says in *Yellow Sky* (1948), as Gregory Peck and his men, after a long trek across the salt flats, pull into a tumbledown ruin of a place, a phantom community inhabited only by Anne Baxter and her grandpa. Philip French, in his book on the western, suggests that the ghost town is an objective correlative for the "impermanence of American life, a pessimistic feeling about the fragility of American civilization and its problems in putting down roots." Jean Gili, in *Le Western*, says much the same when he remarks that what is compelling about the ghost town in westerns is not the absence of people—westerns are full, so to speak, of the absence of people—but the failure of community. A town was here, and now it isn't, the enterprise of founding a society crumbled and died here. Yet there is no nostalgia expended in this direction, no sense of wishing society to fail, which might well go with the regrets the successful society provokes. The western, once again, is not rejecting civilization. It is scared and saddened by these sites, memorials of civilization's too early collapse. But it can't welcome full-blown civilization either. Its true home is that dusty street, those few unstable buildings, the place where the stage pulls in. And the railway station, to indulge in a piece of structuralist symmetry for a moment, stands in perfect opposition to the ghost town. The spot where civilization fails is answered by the spot where isolation ends, where the great world links up with the little town. The train is the world, and the Fall takes place when we exchange our informal relations with the people we know in that shabby township for a set of formal relations with people we don't know at all.

If that sounds like an old populist daydream, we should remember what the township was like before the law came. There is nothing simple about the central nostalgia of westerns. Rousseau's natural man has disappeared from these American scenes, has been replaced by killers and brawlers who need the hand of society to calm them down. The pathos in westerns comes from the heaviness and lack of discrimination with which society's hand falls, driving out John Wayne along with Randolph Scott, cherished heroes along with hated villains. We all lose; and we have no choice but to lose.

But the West has one last, glowing card up its sleeve: all that space (especially in technicolor and on a wide screen), those vast, empty landscapes—all invitations to loneliness. In the attraction of those images, in the lure of that invitation, a great deal of what I have been trying to discuss in this chapter comes together and is cancelled: hankerings for a lost innocence and for a forfeited individualism combined with a sense of the inevitable encroachments of civilization; dreams of a justified, glorified, sanctified selfishness paired with extravagantly selfless gestures; fears of entanglement matched by a clear need of others. For loneliness here is not just one of the poles of these arguments, it is the argument's end, its lapse into silence. In these solitary spaces neither self nor society has any claims on you. The plain and the prairie and the mountain, enlarged and depopulated by the movie camera, offer a life without others, a life with no one, a pacified life in which even your own ego scarcely lifts its voice above a whisper.

III

The Blame on Mame

"Her untitled mamafesta . . ."
James Joyce,
Finnegans Wake

THE SYMBOLISM is enough to frighten off any but the most intrepid Freudians: the bomb dropped on Bikini was called Gilda and had a picture of Rita Hayworth painted on it. The phallic agent of destruction underwent a sex change, and the delight and terror of our new power were channeled into an old and familiar story: our fear and love of women. We got rid of guilt, too: If women are always to blame, starting with Eve perhaps, or Mother Nature, then men can't be to blame. And in any case, as every steady moviegoer knows, women themselves aren't really to blame either, because they can't help it. Sirens all, they sing men to their doom (sometimes doom is just domesticity), without meaning any harm. In Rita Hayworth's song in *Gilda* (1946), a girl is said to have burned Chicago down, to have started an earthquake in San Francisco, and to have caused Manhattan to freeze over, and the refrain, with a cheerful, sardonic acceptance of these and other inflated indictments, repeats "Put the blame on Mame, boys, Put the blame on Mame . . ." *

"Statistics show," a character says in *Gilda*, "that there are more women in the world than anything else—except insects." There is an odd forerunner in the movie of the link between Rita and the bomb—a subliminal *source* of the link, perhaps. Glenn Ford, Hayworth, and George Macready drink a toast to themselves, to the three of them, echoing a toast Ford and Macready have already offered, without Hayworth, "to the three of us"—that is, to Ford, to Macready, and to Macready's sword cane, which helped save Ford's life. A sword cane is like a woman, Macready says, because it seems to be one thing and becomes another before your eyes, but we can all think of more urgent resemblances. Swords and women are lethal, in this mythology; and swords, like bombs, are instruments of aggression shaped like emblems of virility. We give our aggression to women, in an almost schizophrenic separation of the capacity to kill from its mortal consequences. For women, of course, as I shall explain more fully a little later, are also our consciences; they are natural liberals. They can have it all: the guilt and the worry of finding a right response to the guilt. We, meanwhile, must get back to playing with our murderous toys.

Gilda, directed by Charles Vidor, certainly doesn't en-

---

* From "Put the Blame on Mame." Words and music by Allan Roberts and Doris Fisher. © Copyright 1946 by MCA Music, a Division of MCA, Inc. U.S. © copyright renewed 1974; assigned to Doris Fisher Music Corp. and Allan Roberts Music Co. Reprinted by permission of the publishers, Doris Fisher Music Corp., Allan Roberts Music Co., MCA Music, and Leeds Music, Ltd. All Rights Reserved.

Gilda: Guilt galore—Rita Hayworth puts the blame on Mame.
Culver Pictures.

dorse all this chauvinism. It is a tough and impressive movie about what such chauvinism does to people, especially when its victims accept its essential premises. Ford and Hayworth are lovers who have parted. Both are bitter and unforgiving about the way things went, and both are positively driven by what they now think is their hatred for each other. They meet up again when Hayworth marries Ford's boss and savior, Macready, head of a gambling casino in Argentina and secret chief of a tungsten combine. Ford is given the tasks of spying on Hayworth on Macready's behalf and of taking her places and picking her up, like laundry, as he says. "Johnny takes care of all the things that belong to me," Macready murmurs suavely. This is tortured male supremacy with a vengeance: A man is employed as watchdog over the virtue of the woman he can't admit he loves, *for someone else's sake*. In fact, both Ford and Hayworth are trapped in a view of women as feral creatures of lust; avid, insatiable beasts straight out of Boccaccio or Ariosto. Macready seems to die (but doesn't really) and Ford marries Hayworth, but all he can do with her is lock her up and have her trailed ("Buenos Aires was her own private prison," he says on the sound track at one point), and all she can do in reply is confirm his nasty suspicions of her in outrageous travesty, playing the whore because he thinks she is one. "Didn't you hear about me?" she asks. "If I had been a ranch, they'd have named me the Bar-Nothing." Before we even see Hayworth in the movie, her husband calls up the stairs to her, asking, "Gilda, are you decent?" meaning does she have enough clothes on to receive visitors. "Me?" she says, still out of sight. "Sure I'm decent." But the radio in her room is softly playing "Put the blame on Mame," and the question of how decent she is hangs over the whole movie, which does a marvelous job of having things both ways. She *is* decent, we learn at the end, she never really was the tramp she pretended to be—she was just out to annoy Ford. Yet before we learned this, we thought she was wild through excess of sorrow, chasing so many men because she couldn't have the one man she wanted (Ford, of course). Both interpretations make sense, although Hayworth's air of promiscuity is perhaps a bit too convincing to be straightened out by a few words in the script, and in fact I think we tend to believe both, throwing logic to the winds. She is and she is not "decent"—after all, this is precisely the sort of double possibility that movies so often deal in. Both views make Ford the center of Hayworth's life, the one true public for all her displays of talent and sensuality; just as she, of course, is the center of his, the bird he builds his cage for, the only reason for his furious, prurient morality. Men, it seems, have to be masters and women have no choice but to be slaves. In among the complicated twists of a forties thriller (wonderfully executed anyway), *Gilda* offers as sour and as lucid a picture of romantic love as Hollywood has ever given us.

Not sour and lucid enough, though. For in the end *Gilda* became a spectacular instance of the myth it had shown to be so horrible: hence the name on the bomb. The very qualities of the film—Ford's fine air of suppressed rage, Macready's smoothly irritating assumption of superiority, Hayworth's heady blend of recklessness and wit and fear—all fed into the myth. This is the way women are, the film seemed finally to say. So what else can a man do but play the anguished jailer and lion-tamer?

Hayworth herself, a few years later, worrying about her impending marriage to Aly Khan, put the blame on Mame, or at least on Virginia Van Upp, who wrote *Gilda*.

"It's your fault," Bob Thomas reports her as saying. "Because you wrote _Gilda._ And every man I've known has fallen in love with Gilda and wakened with me." Gilda was glamour that couldn't be sustained in the morning light—not morning after morning in any case. But she was also the star of that heroic and much-cherished male dream: the roaring, sexy woman that you alone can conquer and keep. It is one of those dreams that can only crumble. Either way, both you and Gilda lose. If you satisfy her, then she's just another satisfied woman; a wife for God's sake. If you don't, she must be a nymphomaniac.

Gilda's decency, her innocence of all the sins she flaunted, no doubt had much to do with the odd, moralizing logic of the Hays Office: If she wasn't a Bad Woman really, then she didn't have to Pay, and could therefore be spared to start life anew with Glenn Ford. Yet this transparent trick also hints at a complicated truth. Gilda _was_ decent, Rita Hayworth always was decent, somewhere down among the imagery and artillery of lust; but in this role, which consecrated her screen personality—she had appeared previously in _Only Angels Have Wings_ (1939), _Blood and Sand_ (1941), and _Cover Girl_ (1944), among other films, as well as with Fred Astaire in _You'll Never Get Rich_ (1942) and _You Were Never Lovelier_ (1942)—in this role, her decency and innocence took on their final, puzzling form. This was not the generic innocence of women—they're man-eaters but they can't help it—and it was not the later, more vulnerable innocence of Marilyn Monroe, who seemed simply incapable of taking care of herself. Nor was it the innocence of sheer sexuality, which Marilyn also projected so well. On the contrary. Hayworth was not an unthinking carnivore; in fact, she always seemed rather distressed by the havoc she was causing around her. No one as self-possessed as she invariably was could ever seem exactly vulnerable, and she did nothing at all to make sex seem innocent, because she was too busy making it seem luminously, gaudily guilty. Still, as a half-reluctant agent of ruin, a woman poised even in her moments of panic, a vehicle for the vicarious fleshly impulses of a whole decade, she remained strangely aloof from it all. She seemed in the clear, not really compromised by the company she kept or the shows she put on.

The simple reason for this is probably that she was not a great actress, that she held a great deal of herself back from her roles, and what I am calling innocence was a sort of reserve, either an unwillingness or an inability to tap stronger sources of personal emotion. There was always something wooden about the supposedly more fulsome parts of her performances, something slightly synthetic even about the sensuality—I could believe that Gilda was sleeping around with a lot of men, but her motive would be boredom or mischief or despair, not an imperious sexual desire. There was a faint knowingness in Hayworth's face, a life in the eyes and the mouth that was denied to the gyrating body, the supposed focus of all our attention. Still, whatever the reasons, the result was magical: the body was exalted in the person of a woman who clearly had a mind; here was a sex object dissociating herself from all the excitement, and not stupidly or crazily but almost humorously. To be sure, the picture is even more frightening than the portrait of an all-devouring female on the rampage, and most of us may choose not to contemplate it for too long.

Hayworth was simultaneously too ordinary and too beautiful. She was too familiar to be a star. She didn't look different like Garbo or Claudette Colbert, spectacular like

Jane Russell or Jayne Mansfield, distinguished like Grace
Kelly, or magnificent like Ava Gardner. She looked like a
very attractive American woman—even if she started out
in life looking Spanish. She looked like thousands of
American women—only better. And that was the catch.
The face and the figure were too clear and too harmonious
to be true, and this is why she seemed dangerous and
endangered. Her beauty seemed not an exceptional gift
but an accentuation of normal good features into an ideal
form, the sort of poisoned inheritance that could fall to
anyone (beauty, in this story, is a burden that breaks its
possessors; sows catastrophe on all sides). She was an
American beauty who didn't look vulgar (like Betty
Grable), an international star who didn't look foreign (like
Dietrich or Dolores del Rio). She looked homegrown but
classy; she was the real American princess, up from the
streets of New York and the dancing academies of San
Francisco (born Margarita Carmen Cansino in 1918), not
from the best families in Boston, and her marriage to Aly
Khan in 1949 was a conclusive scene in this script: the
American Cinderella, having gotten rid of that talented
pseudo-prince Orson Welles, married her equal at last.
And lived miserably ever after, until she married Dick
Haymes, and lived more miserably still.

For we don't like our real-life fairy tales to turn out
well. We view our most glittering movie-stars with what
Ruth Suckow, as early as 1936, called "a curious mixture
of adulation and a touchy sense that these deities are no
better than the rest of us." Above all, no happier. Hayworth had made a lot of money and was reputed to be as
rich as Aly Khan when she married him. Yet her real
doom was not her wealth, but her perfect, unsurprising
beauty. Like a dream in a popular song, she was too beau-

tiful to last, and too beautiful to be safe. She was Gilda in all her movies, for she was a threat, even when she was doing nothing.

But she was not designing, even when the plot said she was. We can compare her with Corinne Calvet, who looked very much like her, and often imitated her. But there is something broad and scheming about Calvet, her face is full of readable intentions, and that is the difference. Hayworth's face was full of mild mischief, faint pity for us all, and a substantial lack of interest in the whole pantomime.

Welles's *Lady from Shanghai* (1947) owes a lot to *Gilda*, and something to Wilder's *Double Indemnity* (1944), which in turn plays a part in shaping Wilder's own *Sunset Boulevard* (1950). Here are four movies narrated by a male hero in the past tense and in voice-over on the sound track: four remembered excursions into deadly worlds dominated by women, trips to the American Venusberg. Welles was actually married to Hayworth at the time of *The Lady from Shanghai*, which ought to make the film something like a preview of *The Misfits* (1961): the husband as director (or writer) parades the wife as heroine, and we all stare into the marriage. Not so. All Welles does, by way of confession, with Hayworth's screen personality is to translate the aura of sex in *Gilda* into mercenary and murderous plotting. Hayworth is out to kill her husband, double-cross her partner-in-crime, and leave Welles, as Michael, the innocent Irish narrator, to take the rap. At least, I think that is what she is out to do, for along with *Mr. Arkadin* (1955) and *The Big Sleep*, *The Lady from Shanghai* is one of the most confusing movies ever made. She is in league, it seems, with every Chinaman in Chinatown, and she is repeatedly associated with Playland in San Francisco, shown as a place of sudden falls, monstrous laughing dolls, and endlessly reflecting and refracting mirrors. It is because this is her universe that the last scenes of the movie make so much sense, and are not merely a final virtuoso flourish on Welles's part (although they are that as well). The truth comes out in a wrecked house of mirrors, and we see that the beckoning horrors of Playland are what the movie has always been about, and that Playland, of course, is a woman. It is a vision of the female as a perilous funfair, an alluring world of toys from which there is no escape, and even though Welles (as Michael) does escape, leaving Hayworth and Everett Sloane (as her husband) dead in the fairground, one feels that he has been lucky rather than successful. Hayworth was mistress of a yacht called *Circe* in the movie; Welles is one of Odysseus's men who miraculously manages to escape before the rest are changed into swine. "Maybe I'll live so long that I'll forget her," Welles croons in his phony Irish brogue. "Maybe I'll die, trying."

It is a cruel portrait of the lethal, all too attractive temptress, and the persistence of Hayworth's decency in this context becomes all the more remarkable. Again, there are no doubt some fairly simple reasons for this state of affairs: Hayworth's acting, as I have already described it, and flaws in the script. Lawrence Alloway, in *Violent America*, remarks that Hayworth is corrupt in the film "but her motives are less clear than the fact of her guilt." I would say that the fact of her guilt is troubled by an odd sense of her innocence. Alloway goes on:

This failure to motivate her character clearly does the film no harm at all; she remains the glamourous cause of a narrative in which explanations are fragmented over different sequences. In other movies of the time, like the 1946 version of *The Killers* or *Out of the Past,* 1947, there is a similar concentration on obscurely motivated but physically irresistible women. . . . Full explanations are withheld, but the attributes are clear: intricate patterns of double cross and sexual mobility. These women seem prompted as much by drifting as by greed, as much by doubt as by ambition.

What is fascinating, even moving, in *The Lady from Shanghai,* is the sense that the Hayworth character really likes Welles, even as she plans to ensnare him. There is an almost maternal tenderness in the way she keeps telling him that he doesn't know how terrible the world is; how terrible she is. "Why should anyone want to live around us?" she asks at one point. Welles and the movie mean *us,* the very rich. But there is an added, powerful suggestion of *us* as the innocent destroyers, the killers who really don't care about killing and can get nothing they want from it. In spite of Welles's insistence on visual and verbal allusions to various cannibalisms of the ocean deep, including a fable about sharks and a scene set in an aquarium, Hayworth doesn't come off as a natural predator, as a successor of all those twenties vamps who seemed to have crept straight out of a parody of *The Origin of Species.* And again, she is not helpless, not in someone else's power or unable to take care of herself. She bleakly chooses her life of crime and duplicity: out of despair, out of sheer dreary lucidity. She embraces treachery in the way that she faked whoredom in *Gilda:* as the only way out of the trap. Except that there is no way out of the trap.

What Hayworth projects, then, what her own acting and the obscurities of her scripts allow her to project so well, is truly neither guilt nor innocence, but an innocence lingering in the midst of guilt; of appearances of guilt, later denied, in *Gilda;* of genuine guilt, oddly mitigated by her unhappiness, in *The Lady from Shanghai*. She is to blame; she is not to blame. Boys.

Alloway's description of "obscurely motivated but physically irresistible women" suggests the source of the power of these figures. Their obscure motivation allows guilt and innocence, sex and decency to exist side by side, without contradiction, because the contraries are never clearly enough defined to clash. Their physical attractions perform much the same double role, making their owners something like the carriers of a terrible disease. They bring death and destruction by their beauty, but they are only messengers, their beauty has merely chosen them for its vehicle. Thus Helen of Troy caused the Trojan War—and was also innocent, just the bearer of those charms that Paris couldn't resist taking home with him. We put all the blame on Mame and still preserve an infantile notion of the purity of womanhood—for the next time, so to speak. *We* in this case, signifying both men and women: the myth has a male point of view, but claims plenty of adherents of both sexes.

What makes Rita Hayworth, and to some extent Ava Gardner, such modern, such American incarnations of the myth is an awareness of themselves as myth. They too are puzzled, we might say, by the obscurity of their motivations, and they also tend to dislike what they do to themselves and others. Their freedom from the myth which they enact is expressed, not in gestures of revolt, but in their distaste for it: in the midst of the myth, they reserve the right to despise it. And this fits well enough with other forms of forties dissatisfaction in the movies. The world, on the whole, remains fixed and unchanging. Within it, a population of very uncertain characters do battle for pieces of chosen ground, or thrash at the bars of their cage, or convert themselves into paradigms of their own misery. In the fifties it was different, for the cage itself was in trouble, as I suggest later in this book.

Rita Hayworth, as Charles Higham notes in his book on Welles, had several screen sisters: Joan Fontaine in *Ivy* (1947), Ann Todd in *So Evil My Love* (1948), Gene Tierney in *Leave Her to Heaven* (1945). We can continue the list from Higham's and Joel Greenberg's *Hollywood in the Forties:* Joan Bennett in *Woman in the Window* (1944) and *Scarlet Street* (1945); Barbara Stanwyck in *Double Indemnity* (1944) and *The Strange Love of Martha Ivers* (1946); Merle Oberon in *Temptation* (1946); Lana Turner in *The Postman Always Rings Twice* (1946). Possessive, ambitious, destructive, and seductive, these women are all after too much love or too much money, or both. They are usually rather too clearly motivated, are driven by greeds and hungers which are slightly too simple and given, but then oddly enough this excess of motivation functions in much the same way that the lack of it functions in Alloway's analysis. The same "intricate patterns of double cross and sexual mobility" are let loose. Like Hayworth in *The Lady from Shanghai*, several of these women line up allies against their husbands and then turn against these allies once the husband is out of the way, or once the attempt on the husband's life has failed. This switching of criminal allegiances has the effect of an aggressive promiscuity. The double cross *is* sexual mobility, and it is hard not to see in these movies a prolongation of the GI nightmare about the wife who wouldn't wait until the war was over, and in whose case sexual mobility would have to be seen as a double cross.

However, there is no real equivalent in *Ivy* and the rest for Hayworth's indifference and despair, and what is striking about this group of films is the eager materialism of their heroines—a reflection no doubt, as Marjorie Rosen suggests in *Popcorn Venus,* of the new power and the new self-confidence found by women left on their own during the war. In the movies, they wanted luxury, they wanted a better life, and—to the extent that they wanted these things at the expense of men and were ready to kill men to get them—they were in effect the civilian world awaiting the veterans of *The Best Years of Our Lives,* or at least a nightmare version of it, Medea instead of Ariadne, something like a cruel, if unconscious, parody of Cole Porter's "You'd be so nice to come home to."

But then there were women in the movies who specialized in being nice to come home to: Greer Garson and Jane Wyman, and later June Allyson, whose patient waiting always reminds me of that poem by Hardy in which a man feels that his girl is so tolerant of his wanderings that he just doesn't have to go home at all. Barbara Deming describes an interesting sequence recurring in films like *Adventure, Lost Weekend* (1945), *Spellbound* (1945), and *Pride of the Marines.* The heroine is so virtuous that she seems frigid, and other characters in the movie make jokes about this. Then she falls for the hero, and makes very determined advances in his direction which seem to be allowed her only because of her earlier appearance of excessive virtue. And she saves the hero (from wandering, from drink, from psychosis, from self-doubt) against the hero's will. He is always telling her to leave him alone, because he's not worth it, and nothing can really be done for him, and so on, into a full range of insistence on defeat.

Now it is not far-fetched, I think, to see in these ice-maidens, decorously and nobly inflamed by the right man, an inverse echo of Gilda tamed at last; these dogged saviors of fallen men are Gilda's mirror image, violent agents of salvation rather than ruin. I'm not trying to cram all these films into a single pattern, merely to show how they seem to me to be related—and above all to show the *power* all these stories attribute to women.

This must seem paradoxical, since in my last chapter I suggested that women represented society and society was never very convincingly affirmed in Hollywood movies. The contradiction, however, is only apparent. Society rarely comes off as very attractive, simply because the movies throw most of their weight behind a variety of escapes from it. But the activity of women—wrecking homes, making homes, saving heroes, murdering husbands, and double-crossing partners—is so omnipresent in the American cinema that it brings to mind that old joke about the division of labor in a marriage: The husband decides all the big things, like whether the country should declare war or not and who is to be president; and the wife decides the little things, like where they should live, when the husband should change jobs, and how many kids to have. The activity of women in American movies is frequently unhappy and unsuccessful, and often desperate. But it is there, all over the place. Wherever you turn, the blame's on Mame. What's more, the activity of women is virtually the only intelligent activity in the movies, because men never have time to think.

Rita Hayworth, as I have suggested, always seemed conscious of what was going on (in the way that Marilyn Monroe seemed eternally unconscious), and in this she is related to another set of women in the movies: to all those women who think for their men, who guard their consciences, keep them morally up to scratch, and who carry their scruples just as Gilda carried their guilt. In *The Harder They Fall* (1956)—I am reaching now into the fifties, but this characterization of women seems more durable than many others—Bogart is a sports reporter who wants more than a living. He wants more than just "pay," he wants a bank account; so he goes to work for gangster Rod Steiger. "Money's money," he tells himself bravely, "no matter where you get it." But Jan Sterling as his wife simply leaves him until he quits the racket. Which he does, finally, and sits down to compose the searing articles that will lift the lid off Steiger's game and bring him down. As he begins to peck at the typewriter, Sterling makes him a cup of coffee and stands over him, smiling smugly and protectively: another victory for the liberal conscience. Piper Laurie's role in Robert Rossen's *The Hustler* (1961) is as obscurely motivated as Hayworth's in *The Lady from Shanghai*, but in another shade of obscurity. It relies so heavily on our sense of the woman as humanist, as the compassionate advocate of the honorable personal life, that we can scarcely follow her behavior if we don't know the stereotype. Rossen is like those old ladies in Proust who always expressed their gratitude so discreetly and so obliquely that their benefactors never knew when they had been thanked. Laurie is in the movie to oppose George C. Scott and to fight for the soul of Paul Newman; she is generous impulse where Scott is ruthless ambition. This side of the battle almost always falls to women in movies. Men are too busily occupied being the enemy, or the battlefield. Women in movies play the part that students were to take up in real life in the sixties: They represent moral positions that we all more or less endorse but that grown men, for some baffling reason, see as a senti-

mental self-indulgence if they are taken seriously in practice. The best expression I know of this whole trend
comes rather late in its career, but was probably worth
waiting for. In Andrew McLaglen's *The Undefeated* (1970),
John Wayne and Rock Hudson, traveling south of the
border with a wagon train, ride out to parley with an evil-
looking bunch of Mexican desperadoes, all bad teeth and
unpleasant smiles. The conference breaks down, and
Wayne smartly shoots the leader of the bandits before gal-
loping back to join the now besieged company behind
their ring of wagons. A svelte blond widow, heiress to a
hundred well-meaning liberal movie ladies, says, "You
went out there to talk. Why did you have to kill him?"
Wayne sighs, squints inimitably into the middle distance,
and says, "Guess the conversation just kinda . . . dried
up, ma'am."

The joke is on Wayne in the end, though, since this
view of men as too much caught up in their men's jobs to
attend to niggling qualms of conscience ultimately leaves
men with only very specialized, simplified tasks in movies: with men's jobs. Wayne on the range, Scott and Newman in the pool hall, Ford and Macready in a casino,
toasting a swordcane and asserting that women and gambling don't mix, dozens of American heroes at war, Bogart
dabbling in murky Californian crimes or telling Ingrid
Bergman that she can't be any part of what he's got to
do—all these men and many others are in exile from ordinary life. They are in action, and that, in the dispensations of fantasy, is their kingdom. But action appears to
exclude all thought except functional reflection on how to
get out of a tight spot. The sphere of men in the movies is
mostly mindless adventure; intelligence and normality are
the province of women.

What is striking here, and very American, it seems to me, is the total separation of action from thought—to the degree that the two can't live together in the same sex. The assumptions that turn women into the liberal intellectuals of the film universe also turn actual liberal intellectuals, in the minds of many people, into women: effete and ill-informed meddlers in the affairs of real men, do-gooders who just don't know the score. Most cultures I know of suggest, improbably enough, that sensibility is somehow an especially feminine attribute. But only in America, I think, as that once-brave phrase used to go, is it suggested so often that all thinking is best left to the womenfolk. "I reckon," W. C. Fields immortally said, speaking for many men who didn't want to sit around the house and find themselves accidentally using their minds, "I'll go out and milk the elk."

As the dates of my samples indicate, the woman as liberal in the movies lives longer than the woman as destroyer or savior. There is a continuity between the types because they all think—it takes a lot of premeditation to plan a complicated homicide or rescue a man from drink—but it is the continuity, perhaps, of a succession. Women in the movies, like men in the world, seem to be liberals when they can't be anything else, and the principled stances of Sterling and Laurie seem to replace the despair of Rita Hayworth and the malevolent plotting of Barbara Stanwyck. The power is gone, and in the fifties, as Marjorie Rosen points out, women were often excluded from films altogether, or relegated to the sidelines; trapped in marriage or adolescence, in any case. A parlor game: list all the films you can think of whose titles are or contain the names of women, and give dates: *Queen Christina* (1933), *Anna Karenina* (1935), *Camille* (1937); *Susan Lenox*

(1931), *Stella Dallas* (1937), *Mildred Pierce* (1945), *Nora Prentiss* (1947), *Daisy Kenyon* (1947), *Harriet Craig* (1950); *Roberta* (1935), *Ninotchka* (1939), *Rebecca* (1940), *Laura* (1944), *Gilda* (1946). There are lots more. Well, since then there have been *Gigi* (1958), *Gidget* (1959), *Lolita* (1962), *Thoroughly Modern Millie* (1967), and *Who's Afraid of Virginia Woolf?* (1967), but I think the lists speak for themselves (loaded as the second one undoubtedly is). We should probably separate Garbo's films from the game, since she and Dietrich, in their similar and dissimilar ways, both represented the alluring eternal female rather than the threatening contemporary woman as played by Bette Davis or Joan Crawford. The sense of the power of women which we get by adding up very different kinds of movies seems to correspond to a period running from *Gone With The Wind* (1939) to *Sunset Boulevard* (1950) or *All About Eve* (1950)—or if we wish to start further back, from *Jezebel* (1938), or *Stella Dallas* (1937), or *Of Human Bondage* (1934). Before and after this period, women are prizes and trimmings, victims, scapegoats, daughters, mothers and mentors, and number of other things. But they are not, either openly or secretly, running the universe.

What was all this about, and what happened? Fascinating questions, to which I don't really have the answers. It is tempting to see in all this power given to women a massive act of propitiation performed by and for men at the big Hollywood studios. You appease the submerged and oppressed by lending them a huge imaginary authority. And the submerged and oppressed, poor fools, see in these films a confirmation of their hidden hopes and their hidden beliefs. Women do run the world, and always have. It's just that no one notices. I don't think any of this will stick, though, because the women in these movies are only half the picture. The whole picture shows men off on glamorous escapades or helplessly entangled in webs woven by malign (or even benevolent) spiders, while women weave or wait or understand or take the blame. It is a portrait not just of women but of the relation between the sexes—how could a portrait of women, in any case, not also be a portrait of men? Men in this mythology are children—wild, tame, domineering, feeble—and women are their mothers—patient, menacing, domineering, or indulgent. This sounds right, but if we now ask what this monstrous family romance means as a reading of American life, I confess that I think it's time for me to milk the elk, or remind everyone that I am a foreigner. Too many vast and familiar clichés litter the road here: I can't see either the trees or the wood.

But then what happened? How did this imaginary female hegemony come about; and why did it end? It was partly no doubt, as Molly Haskell suggests in *From Reverence to Rape*, a reflection in films of the prestige of female stars in the public eye: sacrificed in the plots of movies, they earned big real-life money and standing, were "catapulted," as Haskell says, "into spheres of power beyond the wildest dreams of most of their sex." We saw fame and fortune where the movies showed us disaster and ruin. But then, women could become stars only because there was a demand for, or at least a willing acceptance of, all those stories of subjection and humiliation, and the explanation begins to turn in a circle. Margaret Thorp, in *America at the Movies*, quotes the Lynds as finding adult females dominating audiences in the thirties, so perhaps there is an echo of that power in these films. Of course, women hardly stopped going to the movies in the fifties.

Perhaps we should look to the war, or the Depression,

for explanations. The war put women in men's jobs, and the murderous wives of the forties, as I have suggested, probably represent a bad dream of soldiers coming home. But the hegemony of women in the movies was well under way before the war. The Depression no doubt made many men feel inadequate and defeated, and there is an obvious attraction, as all anti-Semites know, in finding someone to blame for ills that appear to have no cause: Jezebel and her sorority filled the bill. But then what happened in the fifties? Did we put Communists in the place of women as the monsters we loved to hate? Perhaps we did.

In any case, it seems hard that women should be made to bear the burden of men's impotence in the thirties, if they were going to inherit the burden of men's power in the forties, with the invention of the bomb. Still, anything is possible in the kingdom of myth: all kinds of contraries meet up and change places behind the bland masks of those simple, sentimental movie stories. But then it is because anything is possible that we can't really look for explanations in this area. We can look for descriptions of the many and varied ways in which we vicariously have our cake and eat it, and these descriptions are partial maps of our mind, partial pictures of our world, even—at least of our world as it exists in our representations of it. But for the world itself, we need to consult the more concrete, less accommodating history of jobs, wars, discrimination, and unimagined oppression.

Anyway, there it was. We exchanged Rita Hayworth for Kim Novak, Greer Garson for Doris Day; and we were on the road to the appalling innocence of Marilyn Monroe. If Rita assumed our guilt (we were innocent because she was guilty), Marilyn insured our innocence (we were innocent because she was innocent). Or more precisely, we were guilty because she was innocent, but with that kind of innocence, who wouldn't stumble? She was temptation and pardon all in one, too richly, palely attractive to be resisted, but she was Calypso, not Circe. She was too innocent to exploit us, so innocent that we could hardly feel bad about exploiting her. From the empty-headed blond who trotted into Groucho Marx's office in *Love Happy* (1949), to the haunted creature of *The Misfits*, she carried her purity through all the comedy and all the collapses. The faded voice whispers, the doll face disowns the splendid body, is almost psychotically impervious to all that sexuality below it. The wide eyes blink and squint, in touching, transparent attempts at cunning. A loser. There is a scene in *Some Like It Hot* (1959) which is a kind of paradigm. Marilyn joins Jack Lemmon in a bunk bed. Her breasts swing over him. He sweats. But she's just being nice, and sees nothing, because Jack Lemmon is disguised as a girl. Anything he could do would be a betrayal, but a betrayal would also be perfectly natural.

"She trusted her friends too much and felt betrayed too soon," Marjorie Rosen says. "The one thing in Marilyn we can never forget," Molly Haskell writes, "and perhaps never forgive, is the painful, naked, and embarrassing need for love." Yet she was an invented character. She was the bit-part moved into the center of the stage, the standard dumb broad (which she herself played in her early films) converted into a charming national heroine. Her helplessness was a travesty and a summary of the helplessness of all those characters in the "problem" movies of the fifties, discussed in a later chapter. She couldn't help it, whatever it was.

She and the fifties were a peak in American self-deception; they were a world wiped entirely clean. Not

Some Like It Hot (1959): Appalling innocence—Marilyn Monroe takes away the sins of the world. Culver Pictures.

even Mame was to blame, boys; and not because she was somehow innocent, like Rita Hayworth, or ultimately innocent, like the earlier vamps, but because no one is to blame, and especially not those people who traditionally look as if they might deserve a bit of censure. We were tolerant then. For the whore with the heart of gold we substituted the heart that went whoring, in love with all mankind. We were so guilty that we couldn't bear the thought of guilt in anyone.

IV
Nice Guys Finish Last

> When you're boss, Johnny, you're on your own. You got no friends, only enemies. . . .
>
> Harold Robbins,
> *The Dream Merchants*

> Such was the rule of the sanctuary. A candidate for the priesthood could only succeed to office by slaying the priest, and having slain him, he retained office till he was himself slain by a stronger or craftier. . . .
>
> James G. Frazer,
> *The Golden Bough*

ANYONE who has watched Saturday afternoon television in America will remember those neat and homely little sermons which brighten up the end of sports broadcasts. The camera moves in on our commentator, who slips a hand into the pocket of his blazer, beams broadly, looks as avuncular as he can, and says (if the sport was golf), "Well, that's all folks. See you next week, and until then keep your eye on the ball and follow through." Or (if the sport was motor racing), "See you next week, and until then, take it easy on the curves and keep your brakes in good working order." These friendly, concerned fellows are talking not about golf or motor racing now, but about Life; they are the small-time Billy Grahams of the networks.

Sporting metaphors abound in America; indeed, they are so pervasive that they hardly seem to be metaphors at all. Constant talk of clinches, scores, rain checks, eight balls, striking out—and above all, of winning and losing—creates an impression of ordinary life in America as a strenuous, highly competitive game in progress. Only the game itself is missing. When we are told that the American people have never lost a war, the implied analogy is clearly to an outstanding sporting record. Show me a good loser, people say, and I'll show you a loser—a version of Leo Durocher's immortal precept, "Nice guys finish last." I want to suggest that what all this adds up to is not just a casual plundering of sports and games for a vocabulary we can apply to the moral life, but a popular vision of the moral life itself—specifically, a popular mythology about the nature of success.

I don't know whether Americans really are more competitive than anyone else. In my experience they are no more so than the French or the Mexicans, who are merely competitive in different ways. They *are* more competitive than the English, but then a major English response to the whole of life is a complicated resignation, which makes them something of a special case. What is certain is that Americans love to talk about how competitive they are, and harbor visions of themselves as the most ruthless race

under the sun (as well as the most generous, of course—
but there is only a partial contradiction here, since generosity is the virtue of victors). Richard Rovere, writing
about Senator Joe McCarthy, suggested that Americans
have a special tolerance for "mean, low-down bastards
who win," and linked McCarthy with all those athletes
who rejoice in nicknames like Killer and Slugger. "He
liked to be known as a politician who used his thumbs, his
teeth, and his knees, and I suspect he understood that
there is a place for a few such men in our moral universe."
Rovere's next remark leads directly into the mythology I
am concerned with here: "Our ideas and ideals of sports-
manship may be no lower than those of most people but
they exist in an ambience with our ideas and ideals of success. . . ." Exactly. George Sanders, in *All About Eve*,
sees Anne Baxter's calm nerves on opening night as "the
mark of a true killer." When she appears startled, he offers
a mock-apology: "Did I say killer? I meant champion. I
get my boxing terms mixed."

Success in American movies (and in popular American
novels) is almost invariably linked with an unscrupulous
disregard for decency and fair play, and successful people
are projected as weird, fascinating monsters, King Kongs
of the worlds of business and theater and sport and politics. When Sanders tells Anne Baxter what he and she
have in common, he is defining all the unlovable children
of this myth: "a contempt for humanity, an inability to
love or be loved, insatiable ambition—and talent." The
myth of nice guys finishing last is thus quietly linked to
the myth of how lonely it is at the top. Akim Tamiroff, as
the smiling, moody mobster in *Dangerous to Know* (1938),
soulfully murdering Mozart at the Hammond organ, and
Rod Steiger, as the sinister gangster boss in *The Harder*

They Fall, displaying again and again that childish, help-less charm which makes you almost want to trust this en-tirely untrustworthy character—these figures, along with countless other movie portraits of master criminals who are isolated by the sheer dimensions of their success, are portraits of human mutations. They are monsters who once were men, and those touches of residual humanity remind us of just what has happened: They finished first but they are certainly not nice guys. "I'm sitting on top of the world," Tamiroff says, "and I am not happy." His un-derstanding oriental mistress murmurs, "The top of the world is a lonely place, Steve."

There is obviously a lot of compensation at work in such stories. In a land where talk of success is rampant, here are tales which give you a flattering reason for your failure (you're a nice guy, that's why you're not at the top), and assure you that success only makes a man miser-able. I might add that with a few notorious exceptions a man who insists on seeing himself as a mean, low-down bastard who wins is fairly likely to be a fainthearted loser who can't manage to be as ruthless as he would like. Still, whether as wish or as warning or as consolation, the mon-sters of "making it" exercise considerable attraction—even if that attraction is insistently, almost compulsively de-nied. "You gather I don't like Eve?" Joseph L. Mankie-wicz, writer and director of *All About Eve*, remarked in an interview with Gary Carey. "You're right. I've been there." But the way Mankiewicz talks about Eve, even in the interview, reveals a thoroughgoing fascination with the quasi-allegorical creature he sees in her: "There are Eves afoot in every competitive stratum of our society, wher-ever there's a top you can get to from the bottom. Eves are predatory animals. . . . Eve is everywhere. . . ."

The chief flaw of Budd Schulberg's novel *What Makes Sammy Run?*, which is something like a source book for a lot of these legends, is a failure to find a satisfactory literary form for the cruel and amoral charm of Sammy Glick, which is what makes the novel run. The novel won't quite own up to the nature of its (and our) interest in Sammy. But then it works as well as it does because we *are* interested in Sammy, and we fill in the moral picture. We are all architects and partisans of these myths of ruthless, unhesitating success.

People like Sammy Glick and Eve, while obviously related to those heroes of self I discussed in an earlier chapter, are more powerful and more disturbing than they are because they don't, in the end, even assert the self as a virtue and a value. They don't assert anything except a voracious hunger for success. They have no selves outside of their consuming ambitions; in fact, they *are* their ambitions, and the mythology of nice guys finishing last means that for such ambitions there are no holds barred. You leap beyond good and evil into the pure freedom of a goading, imperious will. These monsters are a warning, perhaps: success, for all its glitter, won't make you happy, so stay away unless you're sure you really want it. But if you are sure, the same argument becomes an extensive permission: you're off the hook, and anything goes.

Occasionally, the monster is reclaimed. In Vincente Minnelli's *The Bad and the Beautiful* (1952), Kirk Douglas's endless aggressions and exploitations all turn out to be good for their victims, who reluctantly admit that they are grateful. But this is clearly a rationalization, a domestication of the superman which rings very hollow. It is ruthlessness itself we wish to see celebrated in such movies, not some purpose to which it can be put, not some hypothetical social usefulness that diligent searchers might find in it. Mankiewicz's Eve, as Mankiewicz himself said in the same interview, wants nothing less than all of whatever there is to be had, and ambition in America could hardly be better defined. Its models are those kings who haunt the movies: the fastest gun in the West, the greatest pool player in America, the best poker player in the country, the heavyweight champion of the world. The best. There is a real riddle here, a sense of desperate ambition as a fundamental American virtue and as a damaging temptation as well. What such stories hardly ever manage to show us is a legitimate, human, orderly ambition, a decent, sporting desire to be the best at something. The suggestion, plainly, is that such a temperate project will get you nowhere, because it won't make you a killer, and if you're not a killer, you won't win.

Nevertheless, for all their fascination, the killers represent, I think, an edge of a myth rather than the myth's center. The myth is a cautionary tale for the ambitious, a consolatory tale for the unsuccessful, and a form of absolution for the ruthless; but above all, like the other myths I consider in this book, it is the semitransparent mask of a contradiction, the means by which the fog lifts over some of our worries and settles again very quickly. It concerns, centrally, not the killer who finishes first, but the nice guy who doesn't want to finish last. It expresses and exercises the conflict in our minds between the heel we feel we ought to be (in order to make it), and the person we know we have to be (in order to be able to live with ourselves for the rest of our days). And in this light, the myth takes two interesting turns: Nice guys finish last is drastically rewritten as nice guys finish dead; and nice guys, especially if they are Glenn Ford or Gary Cooper, or Paul Newman, are magically allowed to finish first, amid vociferous and impressive denials of just this possibility.

There are many movies like *The Big Sleep*, where a nice little guy, preferably played by Elisha Cook, Jr., gets killed because he wanders into the murderous territory of the big time. The self-sacrificing harlot of countless westerns, dying in order to save the hero's life (so that he can marry the boring, virginal lass who's waiting for him), can be seen as an extreme, indeed terminal, case of niceness. Nice guys always finish dead in the West, and the gunfight becomes a remarkable instance of the myth: the metaphorical killers of the sporting world become literal killers on the western street. To be precise, what usually happens in westerns ending with gunfights is that several nice guys finish dead before the principal nice guy, the hero, settles all these scores by drawing faster than the villain. The myth is asserted as a general truth (nice guys do finish dead), and canceled in the particular case (the hero doesn't), and once again we have our cake and eat it. Every western of this type is an exception to the rule it seems to rest on. And the nice guy in any case is now a killer, and how nice can that be—whatever robust standards of niceness you may wish to apply.

The shift from sporting metaphor to lethal reality is underlined by the sense of the game that regularly surrounds gunfights in the movies: lethal or not, this is still a sport too. "Crawford est un sportif," Louis Simonci writes in untranslatable French in *Le Western*, describing Broderick Crawford in *The Fastest Gun Alive* (1956). This particular sportsman has dropped into town to rob a bank, but when he learns there is a fast gun around (Glenn Ford), he has to stay to match himself against him—in spite of the fact that he knows there's a posse hot on his heels. But Ford, although fast, is not really a gunman. He can put a hole through coins flung into the air, and hit a dropped beer glass before it reaches the ground. He even has six notches on his gun. But he has never shot at or killed a man, and he is scared to fight—the gun with the notches is his father's. There is thus an eerie separation of skill with a gun from any of a gun's uses. All Ford can do with a gun is draw and shoot very fast—his skill is only skill, and he races against himself like an athlete racing against the clock.

However, in place of a proud murderous past, the movie supplies Ford with plenty of neuroses. His gun is his identity. "They've got to know who I am, Dora," he tells his wife (Jeanne Crain). Who is he? He's the fastest gun alive, and taunted by the locals and primed with a few drinks, he demonstrates his prowess with the coins and the beer glass, thereby igniting rumors of his talents which will threaten the community, because gunmen will no doubt come thronging in from miles around to test their speed against his. The town is sworn to silence, but word leaks out to Crawford through a child. Crawford himself is in even worse psychological shape than Ford. *His* gun is his virility, his speed with a gun is his consolation for his wife's having run off with another man. None of this low-level Freudian nonsense matters, though, because the gunfight, and the expectation of a gunfight, redeems and cancels everything. When Ford and Crawford step out on to the street, none of these facile motivations counts, all motivations fall away, in fact, because we don't care, in this or any other western, why these men are facing each other between these silent sidewalks. This is the pure, enchanted dream meeting of these movies, the contest for the

The Fastest Gun Alive (1956): Your skill is who you are—Glenn Ford about to show how fast he is. From the MGM release *The Fastest Gun Alive.* © 1956 Loew's, Incorporated.

world championship, the moment at which we assert and then immediately reverse and complicate our idea that nice guys finish dead. *The Fastest Gun Alive* does an especially elaborate dance with this subject. Shots are heard between Ford and Crawford, and we cut swiftly to a grave: Crawford's. That seems all right, but it would have been nice to see him go down. The camera moves sideways to another grave: Ford's. This is not all right at all. Fair, of course, in its way, but against all the rules. The camera then moves up from the grave and we see Ford standing there, alive, smirking. He won the gunfight, but buried the killer in himself; found and discarded his identity in one fell swoop. Practically, of course, he is saving the town by this false burial. Those competitive gunmen are very dangerous: If Crawford's robbing a bank seems antisocial enough, how about his threat to burn the town down if Ford won't come out and face him? Mere greed and thievery seem almost like civic virtues when compared to the sporting instinct.

Robert Aldrich's *Vera Cruz* (1954) is less squeamish about having its nice guy turn into a killer, but then its nice guy is Gary Cooper, and we should not underestimate the distinct and recognizable sets of meanings that particular actors bring to the movies. Cooper carries with him an aura of sanity and decency—how satisfying that he should not like Communism because it didn't seem to him to be on the level—which is a moral guarantee of almost anything he chooses to do; Glenn Ford, on the other hand contributes great washes of torment and strangled repression to any movie he is in. In any case, *Vera Cruz*, like many westerns (like most westerns, according to Philip French), is set in the aftermath of the Civil War, in which killing has not been a matter for the individual conscience.

The complication and uncertainty expressed by the double graves in *The Fastest Gun Alive* are here expressed in the long and appealing run of Burt Lancaster, as a sort of personification of lack of scruples, before he loses to Cooper in the shoot-out. Both men are down in Mexico, looking for loot. But where Lancaster wants the loot for himself, Cooper is a Southern gent ruined in the war, who wants the loot for all those people who are dependent on him. "He likes people," Lancaster says, in a fine line. "You can never count on a man like that."

Everything in the movie suggests that liking people is a crippling infirmity, and Lancaster's own tough-mindedness knows no bounds. He even double-crosses his unscrupulous girlfriend—she just wasn't unscrupulous *enough*—and finally tries to double-cross Cooper. This is his undoing, because the movie neatly inverts all of its implications at this point, and proves the superiority of nice guys after all by having Cooper faster on the draw. Lancaster finishes dead. But then niceness has been asserted only after ruthlessness has received eloquent and attractive and almost unanswerable representation, and we feel that moral magic has been done here, by means of movie conventions (we expect the good guys to win, whatever the force of the case or the probabilities against them), and by means of Cooper himself, one of the very few movie actors who could suggest niceness without suggesting softness. We are close again to the myth of the primacy of the self, except that the focus of *Vera Cruz* is not really Lancaster's self-assertion, but the conventional morality, the morality of nice folks, which he so persuasively undermines. "He likes people. You can never count on a man like that." The thought is not a cynical, simple-minded attack on niceness; it is a wry and seemingly true reflection on just what you can and cannot count on in a rough life. A distorted memory of the pioneer spirit slips into the myth, and joins the chorus of whispers: Nice guys finish last or finish dead.

The gunfight, of course, is one of the most compelling of all the set scenes of the cinema—so compelling that it haunts even conscious attempts to exorcise its charm. *The Law of the Lawless* (1963) has Dale Robertson as a fast gun who has retired, stricken with pity for the widows and children of all the men he killed while still in business. He is a judge now, dedicated to stamping out gunfights all over the territory, and in an impressive last scene, he refuses to fight the man who killed his father; rejects, that is, one of the western's most honored sanctions for revenge. In a remarkable speech, he challenges the killer to shoot him, although he has no gun, because the man has killed a lot of people he knew were not as fast as he was, and who therefore were effectively unarmed. So far so good: a tame western, but decent sentiments. Yet earlier in the film the gunfight has crept back in disguise, sneaked in among that reforming zeal. Dale Robertson, as the judge who has never let an indicted gunfighter get away with his life, faces the ace lawyer who has never lost a case. It is the world championship again. The street has infiltrated the courtroom.

I don't pretend to understand all the attraction of the western gunfight—especially its attraction for peaceful souls like myself—and I don't want to suggest that gunfights belong only to the mythology of success. They must belong to several other mythologies as well, and even the sense of the gunfight that is clearest to me is only indirectly linked to the idea of making it. I mean that the gunfight is a sort of final metaphor for sport itself, a diagram of what sport looks like at the end of its logical road. I mean not that all sport is implicitly or figuratively a form of killing, but that our lives are the highest stake we have to wager. The gunfight is a simplified and terminal game of poker. For an interesting, inverse connection between these ideas, we can look at William Wyler's *Ben-Hur* (1959), where Charlton Heston enters a chariot race against Stephen Boyd *instead of* killing him (Boyd has incarcerated Heston's mother and sister, and Heston thinks they are dead). But then Boyd gets killed in the race anyway, and the competition which has led our thoughts away from revenge has also executed the revenge for us. Very neat. The race becomes an unconfessed shoot-out, a duel masked as a game—where the literal shoot-out, of course, is an acknowledged duel, which is also a game.

I do want to point out one further meaning of the western gunfight, though. It makes "killers" into killers; it makes nice guys into murderers; it probes and exploits some of the stranger corners of our enjoyment of sport. But it also evokes, repeatedly and unforgettably, the anxiety of power. When Jimmy Ringo dies, in *The Gunfighter* (1950), he leaves an intolerable legacy to his young killer— "the deadly curse," as Philip French puts it, "of being the fastest gun around." Or the fastest gun, as the other favorite phrase has it, alive; and we should not miss the sinister overtones in that last word. You are alive in this game only as long as you are the fastest, and your reputation for speed does nothing to help you stay alive, since that is what brings gunmen in from all over the West, trundling in like medieval knights assembling for a joust. Except that here the joust is always mortal. You die on a street, or you inherit a mantle which sooner or later you will die trying to wear, like one of those unfortunate kings in Frazer's *Golden Bough.*

Fenin and Everson suggest that this theme first appears in westerns in 1950, with the film I have just mentioned; it certainly appears again and again throughout the fifties. If it is true that it appears only in the fifties, or not until the fifties, then the connection with American concern about the situation of America in the world seems inescapable. We won the war, we saved the sanctuary. But now we must prowl like policemen, waiting for our inevitable enemy and would-be successor to strike. The Rosenbergs lurk in Frazer's grove at Aricia. At any rate the Cold War often looked like an advance in slow motion down an unending western street, and the anxiety of power is a clear feature of the mythology of success. For a major price of success, in the myth, is having to live with it.

It is time, perhaps, to turn to more explicit, less submerged treatments of the myth. Just as sport is a favorite source of American metaphor for success, so American movies offer some exceptional explorations of success in sport. Pool and poker are the authentic, compelling subjects of *The Hustler* and *The Cincinnati Kid* (1965). But then metaphor and reality are so entangled here that we can't have one, it seems, without the other, and both of these films are also very clearly about the high cost of winning anything: pool and poker stand for whatever it is we want very badly to win. What is fascinating about these movies is that they emphatically proclaim that the cost is too high but can't propose with any conviction that we should stop

The Hustler (1961): Great skill breeds great ambition—Paul Newman hits a winning streak. Courtesy Twentieth Century-Fox. © 1961 Rossen Enterprises, Inc., and Twentieth Century-Fox Film Corporation. All Rights Reserved.

trying to win. The contradiction at the heart of the myth of ruthless success is thus having a field day.

The Hustler is a very confused movie, unsatisfactory in many ways, mainly because it can't connect the story of Piper Laurie as a lame, despairing girl, the figure of life's born loser, with the story of Paul Newman, the hustler, a loser of a different kind altogether. Newman is an artist at pool, a show-off, a dilettante. He beats the great Minnesota Fats (Jackie Gleason) and then throws the game away. Laurie doesn't want to play any games at all. "We have a contract of depravity," she writes of her affair with Newman. "All we have to do is pull a blind down." But depravity has nothing to do with Newman's problem, and neither have the words which Laurie scribbles on a mirror in lipstick before her suicide: "perverted, twisted, crippled." That's her problem, and another way of describing the film's confusion would be to say it tries to crowd too many meanings into the simple metaphor of winning and losing. Newman and Laurie, and George C. Scott, as the gambler who backs (and wants to own) Newman, are all losers in one way or another (and all winners too, for that matter); but merely meeting up in the language of the screenplay is not enough to hold them together.

Nevertheless, *The Hustler* is a very great movie, in my view, partly because its confusion keeps its rich themes alive, where a tighter vision would have cramped or mangled them, and partly because of Rossen's wonderful use of Cinemascope (in black and white) to create an oppressive, elongated world in which ceilings always seem terribly low, and people terribly separate from each other; in one shot Newman is even separated from his own image in a mirror by almost the whole width of a very wide screen. It is a world in which the pool table seems the one natural shape, while human beings seem untidy intruders, and that, of course, is the film's chief concern: the human cost of being the greatest pool player in America.

Jackie Gleason, someone says, is the best in the country. "No, he ain't," Newman says, grinning. "I am." Newman plays Gleason, is 18,000 dollars ahead, then fails to show the staying power of a real champion. Gleason washes his hands, combs his hair, puts his jacket back on, and returns to the game looking spruce, while Newman, getting drunk on bourbon, laughs himself silly at these antics. Gleason then proceeds to beat him in a brisk, businesslike manner. Winning, it seems, is knowing when to quit, and hygiene is a part of success: How you look has an effect on how you feel. This much is clear, but the movie abounds in further explanations for Newman's failure to stay ahead. He is a "born loser," George C. Scott tells him. He didn't really want to win, and that's why he was drinking so much. "If you start drinking whisky gambling, you have an excuse for losing." Scott also suggests that it takes more than talent to be a real winner: it takes character. Another sequence in the movie shows Newman, trying to pick up a little money, playing in a small-time pool hall. He just can't resist the temptation to let the local hoodlums know how good he is. They beat him up and break his thumbs. All right, Newman has the skill, but not the temperament of a champion, but the film is going curiously astray. A question about the cost of making it has turned into a diagnosis of failure (and therefore, implicitly, into an apology for success). What to do. Since Scott's arguments about talent and character are unanswerable, and since Scott is probably right about Newman's not really wanting to win (in spite of his talk about having come to Pittsburgh all the way from California just to "get" Gleason), the movie smartly turns from what Scott says to Scott himself, and makes him a smug arch-villain, an embodiment of every ugly aspect of ambition, a leering proof that you're not a nice guy if you finish first, and you're not all that nice if you even want to.

Newman wants to "win before anything else," Rossen later said of his character. "That is his tragedy." But Rossen must have been thinking of the myth rather than his movie, which simply transfers Newman's wanting to win to Scott. Scott becomes the ambition Newman doesn't have (but ought to have so that the movie can criticize it). Scott lies to Laurie, sleeps with her, and tilts her into suicide. He is the killer, the monster, the cousin of Sammy Glick and Mankiewicz's Eve, and when Newman, at the end of the film, tells him that he (Scott) is a loser (echoing and reversing Scott's earlier line to Newman), he means Scott is a loser, morally, because all he wants out of life is to win. In comparison, Newman's not really want-ing to win at all seems positively saintly, and the movie ends in a blaze of righteousness. Newman's broken thumbs and his anguish over Laurie's death are the em-blems of his humanity. "I sure got character now," he sneers. But he hasn't. What he has is rage, and in his rage he beats Gleason hands down. He is the best pool player in the country, but he is still not a cool professional, and in what is perhaps the movie's finest touch, he is in any case out of the game now. Because of his disagreement with Scott, he will never be able to play pool in the big leagues again. This seems sad enough, although critics have objected to the "happy ending" of the film—they mean Newman's winning, not his banishment from pool. In fact, the victory and the banishment together add up to the perfect, complex, painful solution to the problem that has dogged Newman through the movie, the pool player's version of the anxiety of power, an echo of the fast gun's worry about the next fast gun. Beating Gleason and then throwing the game away, Newman was a man who wanted to win without assuming the winner's crown, and it is just this elegant condition that the end of the movie provides for him. He is a king without a kingdom, and his exile is the price he pays for not having to fear any future deposition.

Ruthless ambition is thus indicted, and the hero exempted magically from the indictment, even from the consequences of success. But in spite of all the criticism aimed at success in movies like *The Hustler*, in spite of the parading of monsters in *All About Eve* and many gangster movies, there remains the enormous lure of success itself, especially when associated with extraordinary skills (pool, gunplay, poker). To put the whole thing clumsily, the suggestion that you can't win without being a killer is followed by the perception that you can't be a killer without killing someone; but then this perception is blurred, almost annulled, by the sheer fascination of the killing. We don't question any of the assumptions here. We agree that nice guys finish last (or dead), and we agree that this is a sad state of moral affairs. But we can't shed our longing to finish first, to be the best, and we can't deny the excitement of seeing someone else arrive at those heights. The result is a sense of adventure muddied by a faint sense of guilt, and of course it is essential to the mythological function of these stories that they should not be disentangled as I am disentangling them here. These conflicting responses need to peep out into the light but still remain mostly in the shadow. The figures of Jackie Gleason in *The Hustler* and Edward G. Robinson in *The Cincinnati Kid* represent this ambivalence very well. Although they are the greatest pool (poker) players in the country—at least Gleason is until Newman beats him—they are clearly not monsters, merely champions, masters of the skills of their games and of themselves. Where the heroes of westerns are exceptions to a general rule (they are nice guys but they don't finish dead), the men the heroes have to beat in these movies seem to be free from the moral constrictions which tie up the heroes (they have finished first but they are still nice guys). They are the pure thrill and temptation of difficult success.

But of course it is no longer a question of being a nice guy in the sense that Gary Cooper was a nice guy in *Vera Cruz* ("he likes people"). It is a question of being human in spite of your ambition, or something less then human because of it. Tuesday Weld in *The Cincinnati Kid* tells Steve McQueen about a French film she has seen in which people seemed to care more about their lives than about their honor. She is puzzled, can that be right? Sure, McQueen says. "Well, how come?" "Because it makes sense. What's the use of honor if you're dead?" There is a slightly too artful counterpoint here to the main business of the movie, where McQueen, as the Kid, is tempted to prefer his honor (in the form of a chance to beat Edward G. Robinson at poker and so become the Man, as the jargon has it) to his life (in the form of a future with Tuesday Weld or a girl like her). What is odd and powerful about the movie is that it shares all the contradictions of *The Hustler* even though its point of view sets out to be entirely different. In that ineffable Hollywood way, here are people trying both to make money by revamping an earlier movie (poker instead of pool, what a great idea) and to correct that earlier movie into a sounder moral proposition. Thus the

"happy ending" of *The Hustler* is reversed. Amid all kinds
of Frazerian suggestions that Robinson is past it, that the
King must die, that the Man is going to have to step down
for the Kid (the insistence on the metaphor of generations
is almost intolerable), Robinson reveals himself as not past
it at all but still the king. "As long as I'm around," he tells
McQueen, "you're second-best, and you'd better learn to
live with it." A stern lesson here for America, in 1965.
McQueen steps out on to the streets of New Orleans to
start learning to live with his newfound knowledge, Ray
Charles sings the title song in the sound track, and we are
close to a couple of favorite messages of liberal American
movies: You win when you lose (*Giant*, 1956); you really
win only when you stop competing altogether (*The Set-Up*,
1949). Decent suggestions, and a lot more likable than the
eager thuggery of some American films, and yet in a
movie that has not only made poker seem an irresistibly
compelling game, but has made wanting to be a great
poker player seem just about the most attractive ambition
that anyone could conceive, they are perfectly trivial. *The
Cincinnati Kid*, without being really dishonest, ends up just
where *The Hustler* left us. If winning is made so marvelously appealing, it doesn't matter whether the hero wins
or loses, and it doesn't matter how many subtle and decent
sermons against winning you sneak into the movie. For all
the film's real energies come to it from the myth it sets out
to criticize, and it ends up not as a correction of the myth
but as another fine instance of it. Being the best is such a
domineering American dream that when properly expressed—as it is in images of poker and pool, and boxing,
and gunfights—it simply cancels every consideration I
have raised in this chapter. Nice guys finish last: there is
an apologetic or aggressive tone to the phrase, whether we

interpret it as warning, exoneration, or wish fulfillment; there is a sense that something like this needs to be said. The dream in its most confident forms replaces all this with the masterful facility of another sentiment: I don't care who finished last, just tell me who won. This is another implication of those gunfights in westerns. If you're not the fastest gun alive, you're dead; and surely a great many of our cruelly concentrated demands for excellence find themselves mirrored in that elementary option.

V

The Intrepidation of Dreams

> One great blemish in the popular mind of America, and the prolific parent of an innumerable brood of evils, is Universal Distrust.
>
> Charles Dickens,
> *American Notes*

SHOTS ring out, as they say. A dying man slumps to the floor of a softly lit room and murmurs a woman's name. We hear a car driving off. In a comfortably furnished study we see a murder take place in silhouette, a shadowy figure strung up from the ceiling by another stealthy and shadowy figure. The scene is accompanied by suitably menacing music. A distraught woman, nightmare written all over her face, paces the dark, wet streets of a city, hounded and bewildered by the sound of trams and automobiles, by the sheer presence of people and walls and shops and newsstands. She collapses and is taken to a hospital.

I have described the opening scenes of three Warner Brothers movies of the forties: *Mildred Pierce* (1945), *The Unsuspected* (1947), and *Possessed* (1947), respectively; the first two directed by Michael Curtiz, the third by Curtis Bernhardt. We have entered what Higham and Greenberg, in their *Hollywood in the Forties*, call "the specific ambience of *film noir*," and I must leave further description of the general mood to those masters of the necessary style, a sort of critics' echo to the prose of Raymond Chandler:

A dark street in the early morning hours, splashed with a sudden downpour. Lamps form haloes in the murk. In a walk-up, filled with the intermittent flashing of a neon sign from across the street, a man is waiting to murder or be murdered. . . . Standard lamps fallen on pile carpets, spilling a fan of light about the face of a corpse; interrogation rooms filled with nervous police, the witness framed at their centre under a spotlight; heels clicking along subway or elevated platforms at midnight; cars spanking along canyon roads, with anguished faces beyond the rain-splashed windscreen . . . here is a world where it is always night, always foggy or wet, filled with gunshots and sobs, where men wear turned-down brims on their hats and women loom in fur coats, guns thrust deep into pockets. . . .

Heady stuff. The films themselves are not quite as intense or as romantic as the above evocation suggests; they are rather more choppy and synthetic and awkward. But they do often create something of the atmosphere the quoted passage conjures up, and what interests me here is that with very few exceptions, the atmosphere has proved to be the most enduring part of these films.

Nothing that happens *in* the films quite lives up to the eerie menace contained in the looks of these movies. The stories, the action, the sequences of murder and cover-up, of more murder and chase, leading to a final illumination of what it was all about, seem trivial, a letdown. We are disappointed that such predictable crimes and motives and crack-ups should inhabit this genuinely mysterious universe. It is as if a favorite character in fiction were to be played on the stage by a weary old trouper, a decent and honorable enough actor, but just not what we have always had in mind when we read the book.

There are exceptions, as I say. In *Mildred Pierce* the unrequited love of Joan Crawford for her stuck-up daughter dominates even the film's murky, compelling mood, converting that mood into a metaphor for the stormy, tortured confusion of her feelings. But they are exceptions, and I can make my point best perhaps by turning it around. The other films I have mentioned, even if they are not quite up to their own finest moments, are competent jobs by any standards. But poor films too, like Edward L. Marin's trite and tired *Nocturne* (1946), come to life as soon as they stumble into the visual radius of the films I am thinking of. George Raft goes off to see a photographer who has some information for him. It is one of those situations where we know the photographer will be dead by the time Raft gets there, and there are all the usual ingredients of suspense: How will he have died? How will Raft find him? Above all (in the movies), just what sort of corpse shall we have to look at? Well, we have to look at the legs and feet of a man hanging among some shifting curtains, but the important thing here is the lighting of the whole sequence. It is night and very windy. As Raft prowls around before finding the body, the play of moonlight and shadow, of billowing drapes and dark angles of half-seen pieces of furniture, sets up a sinister, almost poetically threatening effect quite out of proportion to anything else in the movie—and quite different, I might add, from the ordinary suspense of finding bodies in movies and novels. It is an effect which makes this silent, waiting house seem sinister in its own right, independently of any corpses it may contain.

This is a major suggestion of all these films. The set itself falls under suspicion, the decor of thick carpets, cocktail cabinets, deep armchairs and tasteful lamps; the studio streets slick with studio rain. It is a question of camerawork, of lighting and composition of shot, rather than of design. (The reverse is the case in many musicals and epics, for example, where the amount of art and industry invested in infinitesimal amounts of film is staggering—the making of *An American in Paris* (1951), as described in Donald Knox's *The Magic Factory*, is a revelation in this respect.) What is rendered sinister, that is, is a style of contemporary living, the ordinary, relatively plush Hollywood interior, and Hollywood's mimicry of American streets. The sets are the ordinary sets for movies with modern American stories, only infiltrated with doubt and darkness. I don't mean to exaggerate. Murders have got to take place somewhere, and the fact that we know most of these movies are thrillers conditions our response to their physical appearance. We are expecting everything to look slightly creepy. Nevertheless the effects of light and murky shade in these films go well beyond such expectations, infesting even the most innocent scenes with a brooding Expressionist gloom, hinting with a kind of lugubrious joy at the strong possibility that madness and mayhem are the natural denizens of the ordinary places of modern life.

Perhaps a couple of distinctions will help to make this striking effect clearer. It is not a matter of the discovery of something sinister at the heart of the very familiar—a favorite practice of Hitchcock's. There is an empty English street in *The Man Who Knew Too Much* (1956) that comes to look profoundly disturbing, partly because of hints in the plot about it, but mainly because Hitchcock simply lets his camera linger there. Anything will become sinister if you think there may be something wrong with it, and then keep looking. Its very silence and innocence make it all the more alarming, and Hitchcock has bedeviled empty English streets for me for good: They all look just a touch *too* quiet. Nor is the effect in question that other cherished Hitchcock perception: the sense that famous and familiar spots and occasions (Mount Rushmore, the Albert Hall, a fairground, a tennis match, an open road in the Middle West) are almost *asking* us to get into trouble, since they provide such welcoming and appropriate backdrops for our dangers. Stanley Cavell, thinking of these configurations in Hitchcock, and pursuing an interesting notion of his own (the power of these incidents "depends upon the inflection they give to a familiar environment, above all to a sense that they are as natural to the place as the conventional events we might expect there"), speaks of "a revelation of the familiar." Hitchcock reveals the familiar either by dwelling on its familiarity or by using it as a stage for the extraordinary. But *Possessed* and *The Unsuspected* and the rest of the *films noirs* of the forties undermine the familiar by filling it with shadows. The familiar looks shifty, looks guilty, and not suspiciously innocent as in Hitchcock. It is a world turned chameleon; it has taken on the moral colors of its population. It is a state of mind made visible in furniture and sidewalks, and the question now is what these movies were so eloquently guilty *about*.

The movies themselves were all about greed, of course, about wanting to cash in on a husband's insurance or a ward's inheritance, about wanting to climb into the class of the idle rich; but as I have suggested, the plots of these films were less compelling than their moods, and greed and social ambition are not what speaks in those recurring sets. Or rather they are, but in a curiously subdued and masked way. The sets suggest the contemporary good life. They evoke not exactly high or luxurious living, but just what it means to be solidly well-off: discreet, spacious comfort, the sense of enough money rather than too much. And they evoke cities, of course; the streets are essential to these films. Higham and Greenberg see an unveiling of ugly secrets here, a stripping away of fine smooth facades to reveal monstrosities lurking behind them: "At the gates of the respectable," they say of Siodmak's *Phantom Lady* (1944), "the jungle is already thrusting upwards." This *is* a theme in the movies of the period, although it is more forcefully expressed in the novels of Raymond Chandler, from *The Big Sleep* (1939) to *The Little Sister* (1949), where California always seems about to be overrun by skeletons leaping out of the cupboards of the well-to-do. Ross Macdonald, following Chandler, although he is interested in the past more as a crippling personal legacy than as a fund of social and legal guilt, has a perfect image for the whole setup: an expensive house cantilevered out over a ravine. That is what California looks like in this fiction: success suspended over a big drop.

Nevertheless, this is not quite the impression we get from the carpeted living rooms and glistening sidewalks of the forties. These things are not facades for something else, they are the thing itself. They *are* what the guilt is about. They embody a style of modern urban life which is what we all want (what we all used to want), but the style is subtly tainted by thoughts of what it is likely to cost us to get it. That is, if we want to live like this, we shall have to live *like this;* we shall have the confused and threatened lives of the people in these movies. To put it all a bit too simply and a bit too strongly, here are films that preach, like all thrillers during the reign of the Hays Office, that crime doesn't pay. Simultaneously, they show us what life would look like if crime did pay; and more powerfully and more ominously, they hint that crime, or at least an established acquaintance with terror, is probably the only road to a life like this. And the conclusion of such logic, since crime and the taming of terror are out for most of us, is that this life is out for most of us, simply beyond our grasp. This, of course, is a standard situation in films. Hollywood movies give us our dreams, as the surrealist poet Robert Desnos suggested the movies should, although he had rather a different order of dreams in mind. They show us what we can't have, they present us vicariously with the unavailable. Only here, in these dark films of the forties, the gift is poisoned with a reminder of just how unavailable it is. The good life is seen to be striped with shadows, and although we perhaps don't have much sense of what the shadows mean while we are at the movies, they are unmistakably there for us, converting these comfortable homes and promising streets into a scenery of fear.

This is close to the theme of the previous chapter, where the price of success was thought to be ruthlessness and loneliness. Frazer's edgy king now sits on a sofa in Beverly Hills.

But the real, hidden, half-focused subject of the *film noir*, the scare that lurks in those shadowy sets, is another, less well known American worry, a feature of the forties as much as the Warner Brothers thrillers themselves. I am referring to the experience of class, the sense of America, proverbially open and unsnobbish, as a place of high walls and closed doors. One might speculate that the wartime lessons of class learned in Europe equipped Americans to recognize that social ogre at home when they got back. Perhaps it was simply that with the Depression and the war over, the pursuit of happiness still seemed terribly slow and hard, considering that the major obstacles were supposed to be out of the way.

Of course class in the *film noir* was largely a question of money: of inaccessible money. The genre evoked a nation of urchins with their faces pressed against the windows of the comfortable life. And class, strictly speaking, usually implies the reverse: a distinction that money can't buy, or even more frequently, a lack of distinction that money can do nothing about. But times change. The very rich in thirties movies were different from us, just as Fitzgerald suggested they always were; a topic for brittle, lighthearted comedy and fantasy, a set of funny people hampered by all kinds of ludicrous manners and prohibitions, not a social class at all really, but rather something between a zoo and a comic royal family. By the forties, though, they were the object of a nagging, eager resentment, which extended even to the fairly rich and only just rich too. Class *was* money, or near enough.

There is an interesting progression from *Now Voyager* (1942), for example, to *Mildred Pierce* (1945) and *Night Song* (1947), which takes us from sentimental melodrama into the orbit of the *film noir* and then out again into fairy tale. The first of these films links high social class—Bette Davis as the unmarried daughter of one of the best Boston families—with strangling inhibitions; the film then links pleasure, in the shape of a night in Rio with Paul Henreid, with liberation and health. The film's main concern is a

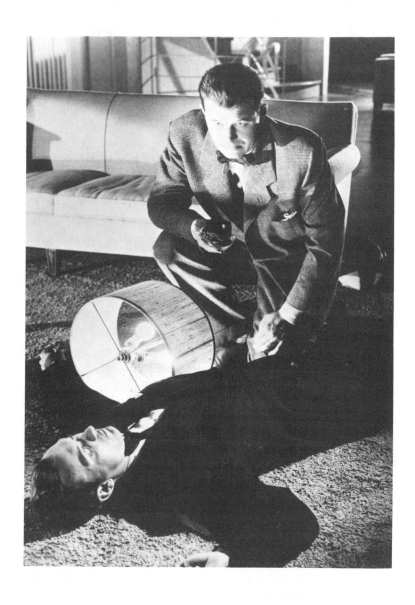

Mildred Pierce (1945): Appearances deceive—Jack Carson is *not* Zachary Scott's murderer. Copyright © 1945 Warner Bros. Pictures, Inc. Renewed 1972.

lavish and sentimental celebration of letting people do what they like—all figures of authority, even persons who temporarily assume authority, become disagreeable, the enemy. Your inhibitions themselves are the problem, not whatever it is that provokes them. But the social implications remain. Money, class, and repression are defeated by love, pleasure, and self-indulgence.

Not complete self-indulgence: Davis can't marry Henreid because he is already (miserably) married. "But darling," he asks rather crassly, in the movie's last scene, "will you be happy?" Davis shakes her head lightly, and delivers a line to delight all true connoisseurs of genuine rubbish, of rubbish with style: "Let's not ask for the moon. We have the stars." The camera pans smartly to the night sky, where they do indeed, literally, have the stars. Socially the film seems to belong to the thirties, to suggest that the rich and the posh are very unhappy, and who wants to be like that. But there is an edge of worry to it, a fascination with the life of cruises to Brazil and fancy parties in Boston mansions, with proposals of marriage from very wealthy men (turned down, of course), which lends a wishful quality to the problems of these people. The message is not so much that the rich have far more troubles than we do, as that they had better have more troubles than we do, if we are to believe there is any fairness in the world.

With *Mildred Pierce* the social question is out in the open, although it is subtly muffled again by the progress of the film. Joan Crawford has brought up her daughter (Ann Blyth) to aspire to luxury, to play the piano and sing like a lady. When Crawford and her husband separate, she has to work to keep things going (to buy her daughter dresses the girl despises for being so cheap), and she takes a job as a waitress. "Only one thing worried me," Crawford says later. "That one day Veda would find out I was a waitress." She does find out and gives Crawford's waitress outfit to Butterfly McQueen, who helps around the house (either she works for nothing or waitresses were mighty well paid in those parts)—intending to humiliate her mother, of course. And so it continues. Crawford opens her own restaurant, then a chain of restaurants, and she becomes immensely wealthy. But she will never shake off the taint of cooking and commerce that bothers her daughter so much, and the movie, caught up in this rather disturbing portrait of genuine snobbery, of an almost Victorian concern for social origins, suddenly sees an escape route and takes it. Crawford has an affair with Zachary Scott, who not only is not a waiter but doesn't work at all, and this now becomes the issue: the idle rich against the virtuous working world. "You look down on me because I work for a living, don't you?" Crawford says to Scott in a quarrel. He does—and Ann Blyth does too. But then this is scorn in a universe of fancy. Not enough Americans live without working at all for this form of snobbery to lend any real social weight to the movie. Still, we saw the other snobbery before it disappeared, we saw the face of the authentic monster of social class: a girl who found she could not escape her station in life, a daughter who thought her mother would never be good enough for her and a mother who couldn't really say that her daughter was wrong. We were given a sense of society in which certain alluring avenues are closed beyond all appeal. The picture is familiar enough to Europeans; they think it is just the way things are. In Americans, though, bred on a mythology of infinite possibility, the sight of blocked roads can induce something very like despair.

Or at least bitterness, and bitterness is what speaks loudest in *Night Song*. Dana Andrews is a poor blind pianist, and Merle Oberon is a rich young society girl who falls for him. The movie is full of unbearably meaningful lines, like Andrews's saying "Light me a torch, will you?" every time he wants a cigarette; but it separates itself sharply from those films I mentioned earlier (*The Best Years of Our Lives, Pride of the Marines*) where some forms of disablement were metaphors for all forms of maladjustment following the war. Andrews was blinded not in the war, but just after it, when a truck crashed into a drugstore he was sitting in. It could have happened to anyone, and since Oberon has to pretend to be not only blind, but also relatively poor in order to come close to Andrews, it becomes clear that his blindness is simply an intensification of a general civilian unhappiness and poverty. And poverty is not just a lack of money but a state of life and a state of mind, a chronic, un-American condition. Since Andrews is not supposed to know that Oberon is not really blind, the lovers can talk about their past only in terms of their respective bad and good fortune. Oberon's easy existence has been sheltered where Andrews's uphill struggles have all been bleak and exposed. She thinks of rain on the windowpane when she hears music, she says; and he snarls back that he thinks of tramping through a downpour to look for work. She has been rich where he has been poor, safe where he has been in danger, and his being blind where she is only pretending is just one more, parallel statement of the same contrast. Any doubts we may have about the connection between blindness and poverty in the movie are dispersed when we learn that Andrews's blindness is curable, if only he can find the money for the right operation. Blindness *is* poverty, and poverty is the one true, universal disability.

All this is patched up in the film by Oberon's active double life. While she is consoling and inspiring Andrews in her role as the poor blind girl, she is setting up a composition prize in her role as the rich young heiress. Andrews wins the prize with a concerto he has thrown together with her encouragement, and he plays it in New York, Eugene Ormandy conducting, on a bill with Mozart and Beethoven. Meanwhile, though, he has his operation, and meets and sees Oberon as the rich girl, so that she becomes her own rival. Just in time, Andrews saves his soul by dashing off to San Francisco and the girl he thinks is blind. She is waiting for him at the piano. It isn't money and success that count, it's love ("We were two blind people in a city full of eyes," Andrews says to Oberon at one point), but love only just made it, with a little help from its friends. What sticks in one's mind from this movie is Andrews's impressive bitterness, his sense of damaging exclusion. He is rescued from total despair only by the inspired and involuted charity of an eccentric rich girl, and further rescued from heartlessness and selfishness only by the movie's writers, who bundle him off to the West Coast at the right moment. We have merely to imagine a real blind girl waiting for him at the piano instead of the bright-eyed Merle Oberon to see how close this film comes to being very unsettling. Like all fairy tales, it depends on the frog really being a prince (in this case a princess), and not just a poor old frog. And like many fairy tales, it carries a hint of the fragility and inherent improbability of these dispensations, an intimation that one day sooner or later the frog will stubbornly resist the magic and fail to undergo the saving transformation because this time, alas, a frog is all it is.

Still, these movies do retreat into fairy tale or romance; they will not face the visions of society they have conjured up. This is partly because society itself, as I have already suggested, is only a shadowy reality for many Americans, far from being that solid, everlasting, tangible substance that society is for Europeans; and it is partly, as I argue throughout this book, because a major function of popular movies is to avoid facing the bogeys they raise. But it is also because these particular films are too preoccupied with characters lost and astray in America to worry much about America itself. They are concerned with people out to find a place in contemporary life, and nothing separates the forties from the fifties in the movies more clearly than this. Forties characters are trying to fit in, to make it in a world that is either more rigid or more bewildering than they think it ought to be. Their favorite strategy is the criminal shortcut through the thicket and what they learn is that not even that way works. In fifties films people kept asking where *everything* went wrong, and the typical crime was not a cold-blooded murder plotted by Barbara Stanwyck but a muddled manslaughter triggered off by Marlon Brando or a collective killing in the heat of bigoted passion. American movies still didn't see society as a reality, but they saw America. They still evaded the specifically social questions lurking in forties films, but they did this by leaping over them and looking the other way. They exchanged questions of private morality for questions of national morality, leaving matters of class and politics aside. The fifties saw the rise of the theme of the guilty town, as Lawrence Alloway says. But then the whole town was guilty. Where did we all go wrong? A frequent answer, as I try to show later in my chapter on musicals, was to say that nothing had gone wrong, that the only thing wrong with America was this pesky temptation to keep asking what's wrong. But a more general and more enduring answer was contained in the questions themselves. Where did we *all* go wrong? Where did *America* go wrong? Just what seems to be the trouble with the human condition? Questions of such scope have a positively reassuring flavor. "I've worked on a very large canvas," Stanley Kramer told Paul Mayersberg, partly apologizing for his contempt for the particular case. "I have either destroyed the entire world (*On the Beach*), treated the Negro question as if it were one vast problem (*The Defiant Ones*), spoken about the freedom to teach in schools (*Inherit the Wind*) or tried to establish world guilt (*Judgement at Nuremberg*). . . ." That's a large canvas.

I need to take a few steps back toward the *film noir*. I began with sets shot in such a way as to make them look ambivalent and guilty, almost regardless of what happened in them. They were a world of comfort oddly inhabited by anxiety. But that effect, at home in one time and one place, America in the middle and late forties, the work primarily of one studio even, is a local, specific form, it seems to me, of a far more widespread film effect: what I shall call, borrowing a word from a title of Hitchcock's, the suspicion effect—the insinuation of doubt and darkness into the safe, clear realm of physical appearances.

In *Suspicion* (1941), a rather tepid movie apart from its disquieting ending, Cary Grant may or may not have murdered his old pal Nigel Bruce. The clues all seem to suggest he did, and Joan Fontaine, Grant's wife, believes them and is now worried about Grant's designs on her life insurance. Grant and Fontaine drive in a car along a cliff road, the car suddenly twists toward a steep drop, a door opens, we see hands clutching and scrabbling at each other in close-up, then the car stops, and Grant says, "You little fool, you could have killed us." It turns out that he was trying to prevent her from falling to her death rather than trying to do her in. Or was he? He has an explanation for all Fontaine's worries; they turn the car round and go home. We can, if we like, believe that all is well. Grant was an embezzler and a bit of a rake, but only a hysterical woman would think he was a murderer. Such silliness exorcised, we can all breathe again. Except that the crucial close-up of struggling hands tells us nothing at all about what was really happening in the car, about whether Grant was pushing or pulling; and as the car turns from us, Grant's arm, in a wonderfully nasty Hitchcock moment that redeems the whole film, drops heavily around Fontaine's shoulder. We see the gesture from the back. Well, it means affection and love restored, doesn't it? It does unless it means that Grant has plausibly covered up an unsuccessful murder attempt with a set of likely stories, and now has Fontaine comfortably in his clutches for as many leisurely attacks on her life as he needs.

The point is that physical appearances here, on which we rely so much in ordinary life, and which are the very stuff of cinema, are perfectly ambiguous, leaving us quite high and dry about their meaning. Movies deal, by definition, in what we can see and in what can be photographed, and they confer on their subjects the peculiar authority that photographs have in our culture. We judge photographs to be virtually unflawed reproductions of the surfaces of the world, pictures of the world as it really looks, if not as it really is. Hence the feeling of literally overwhelming reality we get from many movies: These are real people in front of a faithful camera, not actors set off from us by footlights and greasepaint and distance. Of course we also know how unreal this reality is. We know not only that any resemblance between most of these characters and stories and our own lives is entirely coincidental, but also that the world they inhabit has been fabricated for the film, concocted in order to be photographed—"a phantom city, phaked of philim pholk," as Joyce said. If they don't wish to disturb us, movies allow this paradox to rest in its normal state of balance: A strong sense of reality is countered by a mild knowledge that it's all made up. We believe our eyes, but we don't believe them absolutely.

But there is a whole range of movies (thrillers and melodramas mostly, although not all thrillers and melodramas fit this category, of course) that specialize in upsetting this balance. These movies introduce something like the idea of an optical illusion into all kinds of areas we thought were visually safe. We sit in the cinema and begin to suspect everything we see—either because the movie is *about* deceptive or ambiguous appearances, or because it keeps alluding to its own fraudulent play with the way things look. Believing our eyes becomes a problem, a trap; a helpless act of faith or a simple impossibility. What we see won't tell us anything (as with the clutching hands in *Suspicion*—or to take another example from the same movie, we can't know just by looking at it whether a glass of milk is poisoned or not). In other cases, what we see can't be true: The hero is caught red-handed at the scene of some horrible crime, for example. Or what we see is so full of hints about how elaborately arranged it is that it seems thoroughly unreliable. The result, whatever form the suspicion takes, is a discreet, disturbing onslaught on the very notion of visual evidence. Thus a frequent and exciting experience in the cinema is an undermining of the experience of cinema. It is as if we were to find in our doctor's waiting room a published indictment of the medical profession, naming our own doctor as a chief agent of whatever was wrong.

The suspicion effect can run from the specific, almost sociological, shiftiness of forties *films noirs* to Hitchcock's general, almost metaphysical, skepticism about appearances. In Hitchcock, as in much science fiction, evil is often entirely plausible, although truth is often literally incredible. Cary Grant in *North by Northwest* (1959) is found with a body in his arms and a knife in his hand; Robert Donat, in *The Thirty-nine Steps* (1935) was caught in much the same way. If looking guilty means anything at all, these men look guilty (they're not, of course). On the other hand, and also in *North by Northwest*, a nonexistent character is given life because he has the appearance of life, or rather because he leaves the traces of life: his name in hotel registers and on flight plans, his suits in closets. Appearances are now no longer ambivalent or inscrutable, as in *Suspicion;* they are positively conspiratorial.

But if appearances ganging up on a man like this create a good plot for a thriller, they also provide a fair definition of the movies themselves: the collusion of appearances. What makes Hitchcock such a profound director is his acute sense of the movies as an art of conjuring, as the trade of illusionists. I don't mean he makes movies about making movies; I mean he exploits with unrivaled talent and unkindness the promise of paranoia inherent in the medium's total reliance on the way things look.

Suspicion (1941): Appearances conspire—Cary Grant brings Joan Fontaine a possibly fatal glass of milk. From the RKO motion picture *Suspicion.* © RKO 1941.

The way to approach Hitchcock, it seems to me, and the way to answer the vexed question of whether he is an artist or not, is to stop looking for individual Hitchcock films that will come up to scratch (most of them don't), and to stop looking, too, for the outline of an *oeuvre* embodying a rich and coherent view of life. Lost causes, vain quests. We should look for *moments* in Hitchcock's work, for those perfect brief emblems of anxiety of which he has given us so many: the carousel in *Strangers on a Train* (1951), the crisscrossed railway lines at the beginning of the same movie, the cutout of the Great Doppo leaping up in the baggage compartment in *The Lady Vanishes* (1938); but there are dozens more, and we all have different preferences. Hitchcock sees the world as a storehouse of natural images for panic, a treasury of allusions to nightmare, and this is partly what Cavell means when he speaks of a revelation of the familiar in Hitchcock. Cary Grant is attacked by a crop-spraying plane in *North by Northwest*, and we think now, Cavell says, that "*Of course* the Great Plains is a region in which men are unprotected from the sky."

Hitchcock's legacy extends to films made by others, like Blake Edwards's stylish *Experiment in Terror* (1962). What could be a more fitting score for all kinds of fears than the sound of a killer with asthma breathing down a telephone? What better place is there for a murderer to meet his end than in the center of an empty baseball park? The authority and eloquence, the slight irony and considerable horror of such images are Hitchcock's bequest to the cinema: enough to make anyone an artist several times over.

Stanley Cavell suggests that "the uncanny is normal experience of film." He is thinking of the feeling of contingency that films often induce, when he states:

The Intrepidation of Dreams

I think everyone knows odd moments in which it seems uncanny that one should find oneself just here now, that one's life should have come to this verge of time and place, that one's history should have unwound to this room, this road, this promontory.

It is an interesting thought, although it seems to correspond simply to a long-standing brand of romantic fiction, which has found its way from novels into the cinema in this century, and the feeling certainly doesn't "underpin all the genres of film," as Cavell suggests it does. The first phrase about the uncanny is very fine, though, and I do think that a visual version of the uncanny is almost a natural temptation of film, that an apprehension of a degree of weirdness in the seen world is what films often gravitate toward. What I mean, I suppose, is that although all good films are made up of well-composed shots, we need only the faintest hint that a shot is a bit *too* well composed to get a sense of something distinctly eerie going on.

I don't profess to understand this, but it seems worth wondering about. Why are there so many mirrors in movies, for example? Why do we so often see a character's face in a looking glass, or reflected in a window or other suitable surface, simultaneously with the back of the same character's head? Why is it that the first appearance of major characters in so many movies is a reflected appearance, rather than a direct confrontation with the camera? I'm not thinking of famous scenes like the shoot-out among mirrors in *The Lady from Shanghai* or Welles walking between infinite visual echoes of himself in *Citizen Kane*. I'm thinking of dozens of forgotten movies that are full of carefully harmonized reflections and double images— movies forgotten generally by the public, and also forgotten by me, because I can remember the mirrors but I can't remember the films. In Fletcher Markle's *The Man With the Cloak* (1951), for example, a movie it turns out I do remember and one that tells the story of a few lost days in the life of Edgar Allan Poe, Joseph Cotten stands at a window in an old house, looking out at Leslie Caron in the street. We see the room he is in, we see his back, we see Caron and the street through the window; but we also see Cotten's face reflected in the window, and we see the whole room, which we have already seen the first time around, so to speak, reflected with it. This kind of effect is not at all exceptional in popular movies, or confined to self-conscious works of art. On the contrary, it is very common, even in the most ephemeral, run-of-the-mill Hollywood jobs.

There are two fairly simple historical reasons for the persistence and the frequency of these effects, effects that tend to disappear from movies in the fifties, and then tend to reappear in the sixties, but as the flamboyant technical behavior of artists, rather than as the regular business of craftsmen. The first reason is the presence in Hollywood of a great many directors who were German or who had worked in Germany, or who had been strongly influenced by those who had worked in Germany: Fritz Lang, of course, but also Robert Siodmak, Otto Preminger, Billy Wilder, Fred Zinnemann, Michael Curtiz, John Brahm, Curtis Bernhardt. The note of muted expressionism in Hollywood movies of the forties was not an accident but a discreet, expatriate version of the real thing, smuggled into safe commercial vehicles. And this leads to the second reason. In lighting and composition, all these European exiles and American apprentices could devote themselves to the most intricate exercises of their skill. And they did; and so did others.

No feeling is more familiar to the fairly attentive moviegoer than a sense of remarkable talents squandered on the elegant appearance of a movie so banal in its human content that it really doesn't matter how it looks. The *auteur* theory is born out of just this sense, although *auteur* critics tend to see individual styles battling against the anonymous movie manners of the big studios where there were probably just directors equipped with large amounts of visual intelligence and about equal amounts of indifference to character and narrative. Still, if André Bazin's famous remarks on the subtleties of Wyler's use of depth of focus in *The Best Years of Our Lives* seem exaggerated when we read them, they become marvelously apt when we see the movie again. Everything that Bazin sees there is really there. Unfortunately the evasive and cozy little tale the rest of us saw in the movie is really there too.

The most trite and sentimental of Hollywood films are often orchestrated with such careful symmetry, are so rife in echoes and prefigurations, reveal such a compulsive attention to symbolic detail, that a literary critic who stumbled on them unawares might think he had entered heaven. But does the public see or care about any of this?

Sometimes these effects presumably work subliminally, after the manner of the verse in verse drama or the imagery in a novel, perhaps. Most of the time they are wasted, failing to get into our minds at any level at all. Whole chunks of these films are thus like those poems that would be terrific if the authors were always available to point out their beauties. (Borges has a fine portrait of such a poet.) Or to take a kinder analogy, they are like medieval cathedral carvings, those triumphs of ingenuity and design seen by no one but God.

However, we all see the visual effects which are my main concern in this chapter. Behind the plots and stars of those Warner Brothers thrillers is a recognizable world, which audiences responded to whether they gave it a name or not. Mirrors and reflections are insistently present in too many movies to remain unnoticed. And Hitchcock (and Welles, and a number of other directors) underline firmly all the appearances they are about to bring under suspicion. Obtrusive or unobtrusive, a great many subtle Hollywood touches stem from the same origin and the same motive: Germany, and the joys of unsung virtuosity. But only the obtrusive touches count here—the ones that are obtrusive enough to be seen—for they are the ones that shake the film universe a little, and deliver us to the uncanny.

There are too many of these touches for me to list or explore them all. Their general effect, as I have suggested, is to make us unsure of what we see. They are an invitation to uncertainty, to a vertigo akin to that of staring at your own name and not recognizing the letters in it as part of any alphabet you have ever learned. The known world disappears. More precisely, it appears in an unnerving disguise, all the more alien for being still the same world. Reflections, for example, remind us of what we normally forget in the cinema, unless we are looking out for it: the location of the camera. They remind us that the camera has to be in a particular place for this effect to be produced, and we are so conscious of such reminders that when we see similar things in ordinary life, neat mirages and visual echoes in car bumpers and store windows, we think: what a shot that would make in a movie. Mirrors themselves in films, apart from the reflections in them, seem to exploit some kind of affinity with the camera, as if all the children of optics were secretly in league against normal vision. Reflections and mirrors both insist not only on the presence of the camera, thereby serving roughly the purpose of intruding narrators in fiction and self-conscious characters on stage, but also on the nature of cameras, on the sort of things cameras are. They are instruments for framing the world, for seeing it in chosen ways, and even without the participation of mirrors, any brilliant shot, as I said earlier, will tend to point us to its source, will tend to play on a sense of the camera's slightly sinister manipulation of appearances. All art shuffles random reality into a semblance of order, and good photographs do this as much as good paintings. But Welles's long swooping takes, Hitchcock's odd jokes with perspective, the dark play of shadows in the films I discussed at the outset of this chapter—these are all flagrant tricks, acts of more or less willful visual violence, assaults on the way things look. And the way things look, under these pressures, is suspicious.

Somewhere between *Mildred Pierce* and *North by Northwest*, between particular American insecurities and universal doubt, there lies one more, once again fairly American worry: the fear that appearances will not stay put long enough, that they shift too fast for them to tell us as much as they should.

As an epigraph to his novel *Mr. Arkadin*, disavowed by Welles, but also a movie of the same name, otherwise known as *Confidential Report*—and even earlier in his film *The Stranger* (1946)—Welles quotes Emerson's famous lines about the transparency of crime:

Commit a crime, and the earth is made of glass. Commit a crime and it is as if a coat of snow fell on the ground. Such as reveals in the woods the track of every partridge and fox and squirrel and mole. You cannot recall the spoken word. You cannot wipe out the foot-track. You cannot draw up the ladder so as to leave no inlet or clue.

Except that you can. People do it all the time, and the pastoral authority of Emerson's language is at war with far from pastoral suspicions. The images hint at the next, all-obliterating snowfall even as they seem to ignore it, and this, it seems to me, is a recurring American preoccupation. It is certainly a favorite theme in Welles. In *The Stranger* a high-ranking ex-Nazi has been careful never to be photographed, but he can't, or won't bother to hide other traces of his former identity, like his passion for old clocks and his anti-Semitic cast of thought. Edward G. Robinson, as the Nazi-hunter, knows he has his man when Welles, as the Nazi, says Marx was not a German but a Jew. Nevertheless, the suspense of Robinson's pursuit of Welles, and Welles's spectacular death impaled on a revolving figure on a clock tower, rest on the powerful mood already created by the troublesome thought that a Nazi could live so long unsuspected in quiet Connecticut, could teach in the local school, and could be married to Loretta Young.

This is close to Hitchcock's portraits of the terrible plausibility of the bad guys, and of course Hitchcock is also interested in disappearing traces, in tracks lost too soon in the snow. We can think of *The Lady Vanishes*, beginning with the title. Before she goes, the lady, Dame

May Whitty, writes her name in the steam on a railway carriage window. We and Margaret Lockwood stare at the name, briefly brought into focus, proof that the lady was here and is now gone. Then the train passes through a tunnel, and the steam and the name have vanished like the lady. Again, Dame May had her special brand of tea brewed for her, a variety drunk, it is boasted, by more than a million Mexicans. Michael Redgrave, who thinks Lockwood is probably hallucinating the whole story, stands in the corridor of the train. A cook throws a pail of rubbish away. A piece of paper is momentarily flattened against the window, the remains of a packet of tea, and Redgrave reads on it a claim about being drunk by more than a million Mexicans. Then the wind snatches this trace away.

Clues in detective novels have a certain stability. Once found they tend to stay found. Clues in the movies tend to evaporate as soon as your back is turned—think of all those corpses that are never there when you go back for them. Like the movies' fondness for mirrors, this plainly has something to do with the medium itself. Films are photographs that move; that disappear, making way for other photographs, and whenever a movie shows a vanishing track of any kind, it borrows a twist of excitement from what is obviously an excursion into imitative form. We don't think about it this way usually, but what is happening in the story is also happening to us in the cinema. We should like to believe Emerson, but the movies themselves keep proving him wrong. There they are, inlets and clues fading before our very eyes.

Still, all movies move, are caught up in time, and *The Lady Vanishes* was made in England, before Hitchcock left the old country. There is nothing peculiarly American here. What is American about Welles's fascination with disappearing traces is its urgency. A vanishing name for Hitchcock is just one more instance of the unreliability of the visible world, and in any case Hitchcock faces all such perturbing prospects with jocular equanimity—none of his films is far removed from comedy. For Welles, a vanishing name is an irreplaceable loss. It is as if he had to test Emerson's faith again and again, check it against his own doubts. Thus a Nazi seems not to leave any clues, but only seems not to, and he is caught in the end. In *Mr. Arkadin* the hero's past is closed, abolished, because anyone who is powerful enough or careful enough can do away with his murky history. But only, the movie says at last, if he can do away with his humanity too. Arkadin cares about his past because he doesn't want his daughter to find out about it. His past is thus still alive in this concern, and he can be tracked down through it. But again, as in *The Stranger*, the possibility of leaving no traces has a suggestively long run before the traces finally turn up.

The subject receives its most famous and least consoling treatment in *Citizen Kane*. Here is a man who leaves tracks in the form of memories in other people's minds, but the tracks are contradictory and lead to no conclusion. There is a major, single trace, the sled bearing the name Rosebud, an emblem, we are meant to believe, of everything that was taken away from Kane as a child, the key to the empty heart that drove Kane to success and brought him at last to loneliness, left him abandoned in his grandiose, echoing palace of mirrors. But then no one *in* the movie catches this clue. We catch it, but who are we? We are ghosts on the wrong side of the celluloid; and in any case was Rosebud really the answer? "I don't think any word explains a man's life," says Thompson, the reporter whose quest for Rosebud has structured the whole film. Whatever Rosebud explains or fails to explain, not even we, the spectral, irrelevant discoverers of this last bit of evidence, see it for long, since the sled is quickly thrown on to a bonfire, and flames eat up the letters of the name.

The Rosebud ending has been much criticized, and Welles himself has shrugged it off as a gimmick ("rather dollar-book Freud"). There is a rather cheap irony in the great secret being revealed just too late for everybody, and I think it is true, as Pauline Kael says, that we tend to believe that Rosebud *is* the key to Kane's life, in spite of Thompson's reservations. Nevertheless, it seems to me that the sight of the name disappearing in the fire speaks to us with a power which simply erases all such objections. It doesn't feel sentimental, or overly ironic, it feels thoroughly distressing, not because the answer has been found too late, but because it has been lost as soon as it has been found. The world of the visible has yielded its prime clue, but the clue scarcely stayed long enough for us to read it: a title card in a silent movie, taken away almost too soon. It is as if we were to see the new, thick snow falling in Emerson's wood.

VI

Ceremonies of Innocence

And roll away the reel world, the reel
world, the reel world!

James Joyce,
Finnegans Wake

THROUGHOUT this book I have argued and assumed
that virtually any Hollywood movie, however trivial, and
whatever its intentions, can be seen as a text for a rather
special kind of social history: the study of what might be
called the back of the American mind, or perhaps the back
of certain states of that mind. But the inverse situation
must surely be much more familiar: Hollywood sets out,
full of unmistakable good will and good faith, to provide a
text in social history, and comes up with snappy entertainment at best, and at worst, an insult to the victims of
whatever plight it undertook to inspect. I want to try to
show not why this should happen, which is fairly obvious, but what it means when it happens so often.

Of course it is clear that we can't have things all ways. If escapist musicals can turn out to be meaningful, it should come as no surprise to find that meaningful movies can turn out to be escapist. Escape is the name of the game—or rather failed *flight*, as I suggested earlier: a dance along the prison walls, waving at all the shackled inmates, rather than a real bid for freedom. We can't read commercial films as wishes, that is, see them as indirect expressions of public needs and concerns, and also blame them for being wishful. No fairy tale can shut out the world altogether. But no fairy tale faithful to its own conventions can accommodate too much of it.

We can object to being given fairy stories at all, certainly, and this is the standard objection to Hollywood's rather nervous sampling of what we mournfully call the real world: that breeding ground of lushes, junkies, delinquents, bigots, brutality and crime; the territory of *Lost Weekend*, *I'll Cry Tomorrow* (1955) and *Days of Wine and Roses* (1962); of *The Man with the Golden Arm* (1955); of *The Wild One* (1953) and *Blackboard Jungle* (1955); of *Crossfire* (1947), *Pinky* (1949) and *No Way Out* (1950); the excuse for a dozen films about the insides of prisons and of many more films about hoodlums of various kinds. Reality is dark and awful, we reckon, and Hollywood picks it up only with gloved hands, then puts it down quickly and runs off into the sunset.

It is true that Hollywood has always been given to playing safe on almost any issue you care to think of—why drive off the customers, after all, by treading on their prejudices? Hollywood, in fact, often looked like a veritable school of evasion, teaching directors how to seem to raise questions they were not raising at all, and how to take on burning questions that were so safe that not even the Daughters of the American Revolution could worry about them. "Stanley Kramer's *Judgment at Nuremberg*," Joan Didion wrote in *Slouching Towards Bethlehem*, "was an intrepid indictment . . . of Nazi war atrocities, about which there would have seemed already to be some consensus." The same director's later *Ship of Fools* (1965), she added, was designed "to register another defiant protest against the National Socialist Party." Molly Haskell, in *From Reverence to Rape*, suggests that the Motion Picture Production Code, as administered by the Hays Office, was not a restraint on real liberties, but an exactly fitting reinforcement of native American prudence and prurience.

Yet however well-founded our suspicions of Hollywood's appearance of social concern, there is no need for us to cave in to such suspicions completely. For we shall miss the simple empirical state of affairs if we do. It seems more than likely that problem movies, over the years, have helped us to understand the "problems" they themselves evaded, and we don't have to look for direct causal consequences of particular films or for equivalents to Zanuck's claim that eleven states (twenty-six in another version) changed their laws regarding mental hospitals as a result of *The Snake Pit* (1948). Such startling success can hardly reflect the normal relation of movies to social reality. Movies are a form of talk, contributions to conversations that will continue when the movies are over, and while talk can have profound and echoing repercussions, it rarely has loud or immediate ones. Even incitements to riot have to be acted on by someone, and *Guess Who's Coming to Dinner* (1967) was not an incitement to riot.

But we do change our minds sometimes, and distant or insipid or forgotten conversations are often an element in these changes. Whatever tolerance and sympathy we now

have for alcoholics and addicts and the rest of that unhappy movie family can't simply be ascribed to the influence of films, of course. Yet it would be absurd to deny
films *any* influence. At the very least they are a part of the
atmosphere we live in, an ingredient of the moral air we
breathe. Hollywood's liberalism, its attempt to grapple
with some of America's internal enemies, was and is, no
doubt, all too timid and discreet, and all too quickly ex-
hausted; but it remains genuine, it seems to me, animated
by an authentic concern. If that concern itself seems
flawed, self-deceiving even in its authenticity, then that is
a question not about Hollywood, but about middle-class
American liberalism in general.

Still, evasions are evasions, and a Hollywood film that
seriously broke out of the circuit of dreams would simultaneously leave the confines of this book and demand another kind of study. Hollywood often approached Problems with rather more fanfare than it approached mere
problems; but then it eluded or disguised them in much
the same way that it eluded or disguised any other piece of
recalcitrant reality. Miscegenation, for example, looms
large in several types of movies, but all it leaves behind is
a trail of very pallid good intentions and a lot of early
deaths.

Jeanne Crain in *Pinky* just calls off her romance with a
white boy; and Dorothy Dandridge just has a lot of sor-
rows in love in her films. But Debra Paget, in *Broken
Arrow* (1950), and Maria Elena Marques, in *Across the Wide
Missouri* (1951), are Indian maidens who marry white men
and die for their pains. In *Colorado Territory* (1949), Joel
McCrea marries that unlikely half-breed Virginia Mayo,
and he gets killed in recompense. As late as 1969, in *Death
of a Gunfighter*, Richard Widmark has scarcely time to

marry his dusky mistress Lena Horne before he breathes his last. And *South Pacific* (1958), to switch the scene a little further west, does its most intricate dance numbers on the subject of race. Color is piffle, Mitzi Gaynor engagingly says, but the movie obviously doesn't think so. While full of the most liberal attitudes on the subject, the movie stays safely away from showing anything resembling miscegenation. John Kerr, who was supposed to marry France Nuyen, is conveniently killed. Rossano Brazzi had been married to a Polynesian woman and has had children by her, which does bother Gaynor, as the little girl from Little Rock. Still, Brazzi himself is Caucasian enough, and his marrying Gaynor is a perfect mythological ending, a wonderful piece of show business *trompe l'oeil*, since we seem actually to be giving our blessing to a mixed marriage as two unmistakably white folks are betrothed before our eyes.

For this is what all these arrangements are about. They are *happy endings*, designed to send us home from the cinema unperturbed. Pauline Kael wrote some years ago that "the motive power behind much of our commercial entertainment is: Give the public a happy ending so they won't have to think about it afterwards." But the public is only partly fooled. Happy endings, like instructions of the judge to strike a remark of Perry Mason's from the record, don't really erase anything. They work, of course, they settle our minds, satisfy our cravings for tidiness and pathos, and send us home happy. But they don't really touch the worries that brought the question of miscegenation, say, into the movies in the first place, worries which have briefly seen the light of day in the form of the mixed couple who nearly made it. Hollywood movies, even problem movies, don't usually mean to trouble us; but

130

they do. They are as bland as they can be, but that is not bland enough, and beneath the comfortable accommodations of their plots lurk stubborn social realities which Hollywood, like most of us, can't quite face and certainly can't make go away.

The question to ask, then, is not whether Hollywood's treatment of problems was mythological or not, but what sort of contribution Hollywood made to the mythology of the problem, or the Problem. The first and overriding suggestion of the myth is that there is only one problem. Racism, drink, drugs, delinquency, lynchings, and the rest: the Problem. It's an absurd view, but it does appear to be Hollywood's working assumption. There is the untroubled ocean of the normal world, and in it, like spots of seaweed or scattered maelstroms, there are problems. What the problems have in common is that they are not clear, calm sea; and for calm sea sailors that is no doubt more than enough. When Kramer worries about having worked on too large a canvas, he says, "I have . . . treated the Negro question as if it were one vast problem," but he is still talking of "the Negro question," and the form of his contrition continues his error. Admittedly, Kramer is not confusing "the Negro question" with half a dozen other questions, and we may even feel, at the going rate of confusion in Hollywood, that he is being very restrained. A few examples selected more or less at random show the Problem changing its masks: the Irish of *The Informer* (1935) and of *Odd Man Out* (1947) become blacks in the remakes of those movies, *Uptight* (1969) and *The Lost Man* (1969); the Jew of Arthur Laurents's stage play becomes a black in Kramer's *Home of the Brave* (1949); the Italians of Mankiewicz's *House of Strangers* (1949) become Indians in *Broken Lance* (1954). Certainly there is a popular principle of economy at work here (never use anything once when you can use it twice), and not only ethnic groups get made over. *Bad Lands* (1939) was *Lost Patrol* (1934) in an earlier life, and *Geronimo* (1939) was *Lives of a Bengal Lancer* (1935). But still, those interchangeable *others* are hard to forget: blacks, Jews, Indians, Italians, the Irish—a composite mob of the humiliated and offended, a negative image of the melting pot—Them—the folks who live under the hill.

There are more unpleasant, more oblique switches. Until recently, Indians in liberal westerns often stood for blacks—as if it weren't enough that lands and lives should be stolen from them, we even stole the Indians' problems. Their authentic grievances and sufferings became a front, a disguise for paleface fears of marauders far closer to home. The Mexicans in *Giant* plainly represent everyone whose face is any darker than Dolores del Rio's, and the film closes on a shot of a brown child and a white child sitting happily together in a playpen, backed, in case we should be dozing off or a bit slow when it comes to symbolism, by a black goat and a white goat peaceably grazing in the garden. The image is as eloquent (and as flat-footed) as Sidney Poitier's being chained to Tony Curtis in *The Defiant Ones* (1958).

There is worse. The murdered Jew in *Crossfire* was a homosexual in the novel the film was made from. Jews, homosexuals: trouble. Homosexuality, in fact, is often vaguely played up in movies before it is allowed to turn into something else. John Cassavetes in *Edge of the City* is a white boy with difficulties. He keeps telephoning his mother, but can't talk to her when she answers. He has seamy-sounding contacts in the world of longshoremen, and a name he mentions when applying for a job produces knowing looks. He can't talk to women but chatters passionately to Sidney Poitier about his older brother. But it's not what you are thinking, it's just that his brother died in a car crash when he, Cassavetes, was driving, and his parents have never forgiven him for it. He's never forgiven himself. And now he is, it turns out, a deserter from the army, and his dad, alas, is a military man. Pauline Kael points out that the same sort of game with homosexuality was played in the advertising for the Anglo-American *The Mark* (1961). There was much talk of "sexual deviation," of "tenuous meetings with women," and of "the one woman" who takes the hero "across the threshold—into manhood." It came as quite a surprise to arrive at the cinema and see this fellow going after little girls.

Perhaps the finest example of this faith in free trade among outsiders is recorded in John Gregory Dunne's *The Studio*. Fred Zinnemann has Toshiro Mifune playing Crazy Horse in a movie he is casting, and now wants what Dunne calls, I hope with irony, "another Oriental" to play Sitting Bull.

"It'll maintain an ethnic balance, Dick," Zinnemann said.

A stricken look crossed [Richard] Zanuck's face. "Jesus, Freddy," he said, "you want us ostracized by the American Indian Association? Those are the two biggest heroes on the history of Indians. And you want Japs to play both of them?"

I don't think we should make too much of the casting of Hollywood movies, of the countless appearances of well-known white actors and actresses in blackface or redface. When Jeanne Crain plays Pinky and Jeff Chandler plays Cochise, there is obviously some murky principle at work that says that we can recognize dignity in blacks and Indians only when white folks dress up and lend a bit of dignity to them. Or to put that more mildly, we can identify with "one of them" only when it's "one of us" in disguise. Having Mel Ferrer and Beatrice Pearson play a black couple in *Lost Boundaries* (1949) makes the question of race just an unfortunate mistake, a sort of clerical error in genetics. We think, as Donald Bogle wryly says in his *Toms, Coons, Mulattoes, Mammies, and Bucks*, "how awful it is that those good white people should have their lives ruined simply because of Negro blood." The list of "actors in redskin" at the back of Ralph and Natasha Friar's *The Only Good Indian* reads like something cooked up by S. J. Perelman on a very good day. It includes, for example: Don Ameche, Anne Bancroft, Lex Barker, Joey Bishop, Cyd Charisse, Tony Curtis, Bebe Daniels, Paulette Goddard, Buddy Hackett, Audrey Hepburn, William Holden, Rock Hudson, Jeffrey Hunter, Bela Lugosi, Larry Parks, William Shatner, Robert Taylor, Robert Wagner, and John Wayne. I haven't seen all the movies in question, but not all of them can be comedies, and such casting suggests not that you can't find the right real Indians for your movies, but that you just don't care *who* plays the Indians. And of course Zinnemann's idea of an ethnic balance rests on an even more insidious indifference or myopia: Japs, Indians, don't they all have those sort of high cheekbones?

Still, all this is just as likely to reflect a true estimate of the poverty of our imaginations as it is to indicate Hollywood's recurring failure of nerve. The life of a casting director can't be easy, and I don't mean to suggest that only Indians should play Sitting Bull, or only Moors should play Othello. I do want to suggest that the picture we get when we put these masks and transferences together is ugly and sinister. Japs are Indians and Indians are blacks; rapists and deserters are queers; queers are Jews; Italians are Indians; blacks used to be Irish or Jewish. It is important for us to see that this universe of metamorphosis is not just a matter of Hollywood's repeatedly exploiting what it takes to be good material, and not just a matter of Hollywood's thinking distress and prejudice are food for a genre rather than facts of life. The notion that all problems can be reduced to a single Problem—that of irksome deviations from normalcy—does not originate in Hollywood and is not confined to the movies. It has its home in many places. It is liberal abstraction at its high point, ethnocentricity in a state of trance: *We are the world,* and anyone who is not just like us becomes a candidate for our pity, a leper of modern life. A good deal of decency goes into such thinking; yet only foggy and cruel condescension comes out.

The mythology of the Problem has many moods and faces, of course, but I wish now to explore a single, recurring feature of serious Hollywood films: the peculiar, almost saintly innocence of the victims of prejudice and hatred.

A trio of innocent men is lynched in William Wellman's *The Ox-Bow Incident,* and Higham and Greenberg suggest that the "anti-lynching argument would surely have been reinforced had one of them been guilty." The Jew who is killed in Edward Dmytryk's *Crossfire* is a veteran with a fine war record, and Higham and Greenberg ask again: "Surely it would still have been wrong to kill him if he had been a draft-dodger, a profiteer, a degenerate?" Stuart

Whitman, in *The Mark,* is a child molester who can't quite bring himself to molest a child on the screen and Pauline Kael nails the film firmly to the wall:

When you think it over, *The Mark* falls apart. You can't help wondering why the film makers have evaded the actual commission of a sex crime: would he (Whitman) somehow not be a suitable subject for a compassionate study if he *had actually* attacked the child? What the movie turns out to be about is a man who has expiated a crime he hasn't committed: in other words, he's morally one up on all of us, and still, he's being branded and mistreated by society. So many of those movies with what purport to be daring themes manage to dodge the issue. In a movie attack on capital punishment the man who is sentenced to death cannot be guilty; in race relations movies, the Negroes and Jews who are mistreated by sadists and bullies are men of such transcendent heroism that they are scarcely recognizable as human beings. We can only assume that if Jews or Negroes are shown as bad-tempered or nasty, or if the boy accused of homosexuality were really guilty of it, the movie would suggest that they should be in the hands of sadists and bullies.

All this seems to me wonderfully sharp and absolutely right. But it also strikes me as a little incurious about what is going on in all these movies. Why *are* those Jews and blacks so nice, why *are* the queers and criminals so pure? Or to sum it up in a question which will cover a number of others, why is the lynched man always innocent?

The lynched man is not always innocent. There is some doubt about him in *They Won't Forget* (1937), and one of the slaughtered thugs in *Try and Get Me* (1951) is a murderer. Nevertheless, the story remains compelling and familiar, from *Fury* (1936) through *The Ox-Bow Incident* and on into all kinds of parallel and related cases. He didn't do it, whatever it was. His innocence is what makes his persecution so terrible.

The Ox-Bow Incident (1943): The good guys look saintly—Dana Andrews, about to be strung up by a lynch mob, writes a philosophical letter to his wife. Courtesy of Twentieth Century-Fox. © 1942 Twentieth Century-Fox Film Corporation. All Rights Reserved.

Certainly this point of view is a complete, if implicit, denial of everything that such films stand for, as Pauline Kael says. If lynching (and all the varieties of prejudice against so-called deviants) can be seen to be wrong only when the victim is innocent, we have no case against lynching (or prejudice) at all. All of these films tend to suggest, against their better intentions, that we are entitled to feed people to the dogs as long as we pick the right people, and *The Ox-Bow Incident* adds an extra twist to this line of thought by having its victims not only innocent of murder, but strung up for a murder that didn't even take place. The man they were supposed to have killed is still alive, and this heavy irony seems to imply not so much that we ought not to lynch people as that we ought to check our facts out properly before we do. There is a weird reversal in *Crossfire* too. This decent and powerful movie about anti-Semitism ends with Robert Young shooting Robert Ryan, the anti-Semite. Ryan is a murderer trying to escape and Young is a detective, but the tone of the conclusion still seems odd. "Is he dead?" someone asks, as Ryan lies there on the floor. And Young, stuffing his gun back into his belt, glibly replies, "He's been dead a long time, only he didn't know it." It's all right to kill killers: the perfect, leaky corollary to the axiom that you mustn't persecute innocent people.

We might say that the victims are innocent in all these movies because that makes the argument more forceful and more dramatic (although it also denatures the argument completely). We might say that only innocent victims are likely to elicit real sympathy from the audience (but then so much the worse for the audience's miserable range of sympathy). We might say that for many hardboiled Americans lynching an innocent man would seem

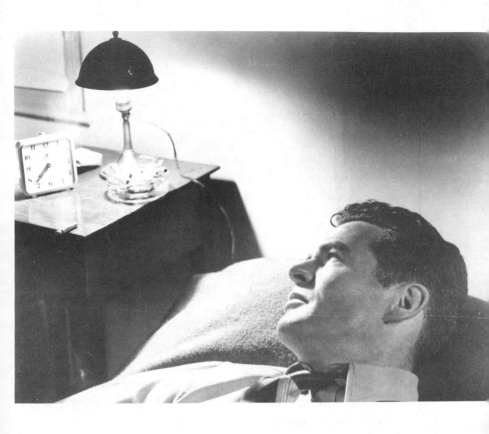

Crossfire (1947): The bad guys look haunted—Robert Ryan, as an anti-Semitic murderer who knows his hours are numbered, waits for the end. From the RKO motion picture *Crossfire*. © RKO 1946.

horrible where lynching a guilty man would seem a mere technical slip (but then those Americans are responding to the idea of error, not to the undesirability of lynchings). None of this sounds very weighty. The innocence of victims stems from the principle that says that victims must be innocent, that unless you are innocent, you are not a victim. If you're guilty, even only slightly, the whole question changes, since merely getting more than your just deserts is plainly a matter of moral accounting rather than a miscarriage of justice. What these movie stories articulate, I think, is a secret affinity with the lynchers that most of us would probably prefer to deny. The lynchers go too far, of course, and they get the wrong man. But if they got the right man, and if they stopped short of killing him, what exactly would be our grief against them?

Somewhere at the back of all this lurks the American weakness for the idea of purity, for the notion of an entirely unflecked innocence. Witch-hunts in America are always pursuits of taints and stains, and J. Parnell Thomas spoke truer (as well as more comically) than he knew when he said in a session of the House Un-American Activities Committee in 1947:

> Once the American people are acquainted with the facts there is no question but what the American people will do the kind of job they want done: that is, to make America just as pure as we can possibly make it.

The unattractive thought that being suspected of something is enough to make you guilty is backed by the equally unattractive thought that if you are guilty you have no rights at all, you simply cease to be a human being. The lynchers steal in on the heels of Joe McCarthy, and instead of defending the guilty, we defend only the innocent. If you are guilty, you should expect to be lynched; and worse still, you would half-suspect the lynchers were right.

Of course, the innocence of victims in the movies often appears to be more a formal question than anything else. Its purpose is to supply Irony, and it is a major category of melodrama's Terrible Mistake, which in turn is Hollywood's formula for skirting tragedy without really looking into its despairing face. In the film version of *Wuthering Heights* (1939) the irreconcilable halves of Catherine Earnshaw's life, her hopeless longing for both Heathcliff and a civilized existence with Edgar Linton, dwindle, in their passage from the novel, as George Bluestone says, into a matter of unfortunate timing. Heathcliff is so slow in going off to make his fortune that Catherine is married to Linton by the time he gets back: cursed bad luck. Similarly, in *Gone With The Wind*, Rhett Butler just doesn't know how much Scarlett loves him, and slopes off into the fog with his luggage. The artist suffers in movies like *A Song to Remember* (1945) and *Rhapsody in Blue* (1945) because, as Pauline Kael says, he doesn't know as much about posterity as we do. It is all a question of fluffed possibilities and almost instant hindsight: melodrama's inverse form of the cavalry rattling in at the last minute. The cavalry arrives a minute too late—literally in the case of the sheriff in *The Ox-Bow Incident*, arriving with the news that there has been no murder. Missing your life or losing it is seen as something like missing a train or losing your footing on a high ledge. There is all the pathos of a ghastly accident; none of the asperity of tragedy. There will be other trains and other ledges—for other people, at any rate. We may have better luck than these unhappy martyrs, fiefs to the whims of Time, scapegoats for our sense that nobody ever seems to understand us and nothing ever seems to go right.

Problem movies, then, owe a double allegiance: to their problem (the Problem) and to their genre, which is a subdivision of melodrama. What is perhaps not too clear at first glance is how severe the rules of the genre can be. The pressures on problem movies to come up with a Big Irony or a Terrible Mistake seem almost greater than the pressures on them not to offend too many people. Or perhaps we should combine these two factors. For the pressures appear to be one and the same: obeying the rules of melodrama is the way you keep from offending people, because you stay within a recognized zone of entertainment. But then not all melodrama insists so much or so nervously on having victims with clean hands.

The lynched man is innocent; the murdered Jew was a hero; and the rapist doesn't actually get to commit a rape. A very intricate game of allusions is being played, a form of charades. Problems are conjured up in *trompe l'oeil*. They seem to be there, but they are not there at all when you look closely: mirages. Innocent and noble and restrained figures stand in for their guilty, infamous, and self-indulgent twins. Yet how can they stand in for characters who are so plainly their opposites? We would be just as sympathetic, of course, to the Hydes of all these Jekylls if they showed their ugly faces, to real murderers and cowards and sexual offenders—except that we know we would not. We are back with the blacks and the Indians played by white actors and actresses—of course no one should discriminate against Jeanne Crain or Mel Ferrer. We find ourselves asserting our tolerance in a situation designed to leave our tolerance completely untested. Hence the remarkable attraction of those stories, and hence the rather smug, self-congratulatory note that often creeps into them.

We are all thoughtful, progressive folks together, and there is a ring of sad truth in David and Evelyn T. Riesman's suggestion that even problem pictures function best as manuals of etiquette, that

audiences at race-relations "problem" films may take the movies, not in terms of getting worked up themselves about racial injustice, but as a cue concerning proper race-relations attitudes in a group in which they may want to move.

Sidney Poitier spoke to Gordon Gow about the assumptions behind a number of these movies.

Now, to film-makers, the Negro is not an oddity. He's not a rarity. They see him every day. . . . They feel they have in their hands the authority and the ability to determine what a film will do. So they say, "Well now, I'm going to make a wonderful humane statement with the presence of this Negro person who has lived under great handicaps and great denial all of his life." So they make a statement. And the statement finally is, "You should be nice to your coloured friends. They too are human beings." Well, this is messy, you know.

It is messy; but it is messy in the way that popular movies usually are. The blurred meanings that give an edge to trivial films remove the edge from films that are trying harder. The innocence of victims in such movies is an alibi for audiences, the means of our cheating entry into the ranks of the concerned and the compassionate. But it is also emblematic of a larger, all-encompassing pardon—of the all-absolving innocence that came to be associated with Marilyn Monroe. As I suggested earlier, this was a cure that spread like a disease, that reached everywhere, like a miracle detergent, scouring guilt from the most unlikely corners. Innocence haunts American movies from the end of the forties—we didn't fall from Paradise, we were pushed. Montgomery Clift as Freud in John Huston's film of that name (1962) stumbles on panics and pathologies that might well lead one to conclude that everyone is guilty, but he quickly settles for a sounder view of things and concludes, unlike Freud as played by Freud himself, that no one is guilty. He was a "strange boy," Robert Taylor's aunt remembers in a film called *The Conspirator* (1949), he had been "too much alone." "I've never had the faintest inkling of what goes on in that restless head of yours," she tells him. And this, we are to understand, is how he became a traitor and a Russian agent: too much alone when he was a boy, not enough love and companionship. All serious human choices vanish in these perspectives. There is no guilt, there are only trains of unhappy circumstance leading to treason (and murder, and prejudice, and drink, and drugs, and delinquency, and attempted rape).

There is a kind of endemic helplessness about the central figures of problem movies. Victims of dope and alcohol are fighting losing battles against their addictions; and even lynch mobs are usually sheepish enough afterwards, aware now of how far they were carried by passions stronger than they were. Delinquents never know what they want or where they are going, and even fairly plausible explanations of what they are after seem too rigid, a straitjacket for longings whose very lack of clear contour is an aspect of their power. A policeman in *The Wild One* says that Brando and his friends are just "looking for somebody to push them around so they can get sore and show how tough they are." That sounds about right to me, but the movie makes it seem to be the simplistic diagnosis of a know-it-all. Anyone who can say what is the matter with these kids cannot, by definition, know what is the matter with them. In this context, it becomes obvious why Brando's and James Dean's mumbling was so much a part of what they had to say. As for blacks, the tone of liberal films is mostly closer to pity than to respect: they can't *help* being black, after all. It's not their fault, and they're in good company, because in these movies, as I say, nothing is anyone's fault. The world is full of uncaused events, littered with things that are just one of those things. We are all wrongly accused. We live inside a curious, sentimental reversal of Kafka's *Trial*, where the *court* is always found to be stacked and guilty. We have been lynched by life. "Wish me luck. I got a raw deal," a tough, embittered woman says in *The Big Sleep*. Bogart, as Philip Marlowe, wiser and stricter and meaner than a problem movie, replies, "Your kind always does."

VII

Darkness in the Dance

Guiltlessness. Our fat Fifties cars, how we loved them, revved them: no thought of pollution. Exhaust smoke, cigarette smoke, factory smoke, all romantic. Romance of consumption at its height. . . . Viewed the world through two lenses since discarded: fear and gratitude . . .

John Updike,
Museums and Women

. . . wide empty grin
that never lost a vote (O Adlai mine).
John Berryman,
The Dream Songs

JUST AS many thrillers offer an outlet for unspecified anxieties, for thoughts of anything we may happen to be anxious about, so the musical can be seen as the vehicle of an all-purpose joy, any joy, the vehicle of anything that makes you feel like singing and dancing. But a basic distinction needs to be made. Many movie musicals, and almost all stage musicals, present the moment of breaking into song and dance as a literal break, a sharp change of gear from the prosaic speech and dull motions of ordinary existence. It doesn't really matter whether this occurs in any given case through highly stylized intentions or common or garden ineptness, since the effect is the same: a clear separation of music from life. You can dance only when Busby Berkeley waves his magic wand, sing only when a clumsy musical cue makes a song inevitable. The lyrical moments of your life take place on a carefully prepared alp, as in *The Sound of Music* (1965), or amid fulsome nostalgia and artifice, as in *Oliver!* (1968) and *The Boy Friend* (1971), or when the plot keeps providing broad excuses, as in *Every Night at Eight* (1935).

The great achievements of the American movie musical propose exactly the reverse of all this. I'm thinking of the films of Fred Astaire and Ginger Rogers, of course, and of the run of musicals produced for MGM by Arthur Freed (*Meet Me in St. Louis*, 1944, *On the Town*, 1949, *An American in Paris*, 1951, *Singin' in the Rain*, 1952, *The Band Wagon*, 1953, and others). The suggestion now is of a genuine continuity between ordinary life and music, a sense of the world as filled with pretexts for song and invitations to the dance. Astaire has his shoes shined to rhythm on Forty-second Street, slips into a natty musical number as he puts on his jacket and tie; Gene Kelly waltzes with mops and gavottes with umbrellas. Of course the rest of us don't literally get quite so carried away, but we might, as we know the feeling that is being so eloquently acted out for us here.

To put it crudely, one kind of musical blatantly puts music where there is none, providing an arrant compensation for a dreary lack of music in our daily doings. The other kind hints that music is everywhere, scattered all about us if we will only look and listen. Astaire and Kelly are the agents of hidden truths rather than pure fantasies, they are our own voices and our own feet, dancing and singing through those times when we really feel that way about our lives.

Both men walk through their movies as if walking could become dancing at any minute: hand in pocket, hat tipped back, reckless and engaging grin, a set of movements well on their way into music. Similarly, their singing voices are not the voices of singers. They are their speaking voices lifted into song, reinforcing the sense of a continuity from talk into lyric, and by extension—or by reversal—a continuity from their lives into ours. We can't sing at all, but if we could, we'd sing like this, not like Nelson Eddy or Mario Lanza.

Beyond this, everything about the two men is different. Their similarities themselves come to mean different things. The moral possibilities incarnate in Fred Astaire are personal, universal, and apparently everlasting, exempt from history and geography. There will always be moments everywhere (I hope) when people will feel that way about their private lives, although, alas, there will not always be Astaire to tap out their feelings for them. Gene Kelly, on the other hand, embodies a public, temporal, American promise, and this is why his movies appear dated in a way that Astaire's never will. To see *Top Hat* (1935) now is to see a film that was always an exercise in nostalgia, even when it was made—a thirties romance of the twenties, as Arlene Croce puts it in her brilliant book on Astaire and Rogers. To see *An American in Paris* is to take off into time-travel, to fall through a time-warp into a lost zone of American confidence and enthusiasm, into a forgotten age of hubris and innocence, one in which David Riesman could write that he thought we were living in "one of the great cultures of history," comparable to the Athens of Pericles. We were certainly about to fight the Peloponnesian War, but that wasn't what Riesman meant. When we hear Kelly's version of "Singin' in the Rain" over the titles of Kubrick's *A Clockwork Orange* (1971), the effect is cruelly, reductively humorous. A man out that late singing these days would be mugged before he got through the first chorus.

Astaire is all wit, grace, skepticism. There is a moment in *Flying Down to Rio* (1933) where he arrives at a ball wearing a top hat and carrying a cane. He looks uncomfortable wearing the hat because it seems almost as big as he is, but then he takes it off and mimes his discomfort with it and with his cane: he doesn't know which of the two stiff-necked waiting attendants is supposed to take these things. His mime of discomfort is so perfectly graceful that all sense of discomfort is canceled. Earlier in the same film, Astaire and Rogers dance the carioca, which is done with the foreheads of the two partners touching. At the end of the number they pretend to crack their heads together, and then stagger about. Their staggering is so elegant and so underplayed that it represents the reverse of clumsiness. Collisions and accidents become a dance, just as discomfort is translated into a joking grace. Social uneasiness is converted into a superior form of social ease, and a (faked) lack of skill becomes supreme skill itself.

Gene Kelly has plenty of skill, but ease is the last thing we associate with him. He does all kinds of difficult numbers, but we are meant to see how difficult they are. His stock-in-trade is drive and buoyancy, an expense of energy and steam which often seems awkward beside Astaire's restraint, but which also makes far more ambitious claims for itself. Fred Astaire is a style, but Gene Kelly is a state of mind, almost an ideology. Astaire is our enduring dream of the effortless conquest of recalcitrant circumstance; Kelly is the indefatigable American, in or out of Paris, he is the practicing apostle of exertion and expertise as keys to fabulous success, and it is the American mood which found its metaphor in Kelly's brash confidence that I now wish to explore a little further.

It was an odd confidence. "I like myself," Kelly sang in *It's Always Fair Weather*, celebrating his victory over self-distrust, and he took the words out of the mouths of many fifties heroes, or rather he said for them what many fifties heroes never quite managed to say on their own. William Holden, Glenn Ford, Montgomery Clift: a generation of actors who specialized in characters who had trouble liking themselves. We liked them, of course; and they usually did all right by the end of the movie. But they never really looked around for reasons to like themselves, and certainly never found any. On the contrary, they applied the opposite principle: like yourself, and the reasons will soon come along. And this is what is odd about the whole mood. It urges not confidence in yourself, or in America, but confidence in confidence—a belated, comic echo to Roosevelt's first inaugural address. If all we had to fear in the thirties was fear itself, all we had to be confident about now, apparently, was confidence. You tell yourself you're living in the Athens of Pericles every morning as you shave. The spirit of Dale Carnegie answers the ghost of Thucydides. As late as 1961, in *The Image*, Daniel Boorstin was suggesting that "our problems arise less from our weaknesses than from our strengths"—a wonderfully illusory notion to be found in a book about dispersing illusions.

It all makes sense, of course. The confidence that was being paraded so bravely was ebbing fast, and soon it was being paraded *because* it was ebbing fast. In the movies, the years of the decline of the great MGM musicals are also the years of the rise of the movies of Marlon Brando and James Dean, and a few dates and titles here make an interesting, even eloquent picture:

1951	*An American in Paris*
1952	*Singin' in the Rain*
1953	*The Wild One*
	The Band Wagon
1954	*On the Waterfront*
1955	*It's Always Fair Weather*
	Guys and Dolls
	East of Eden
	Rebel Without a Cause

If we wish to include the uncertain heroes I've already mentioned, we can add *A Place in the Sun* (1951), with Montgomery Clift, *Blackboard Jungle* (1955), with Glenn Ford, and *Picnic* (1955), with William Holden.

It is not entirely a question of contrasts between the musicals and the melodramas. Kelly's confidence in confidence is echoed in the other films by an insistence on movement for movement's sake. Montgomery Clift can't not want success in *A Place in the Sun*, and thoughts of killing Shelley Winters so that he can marry Elizabeth Taylor are presented as an understandable, almost praiseworthy, obsession: Who wants to marry a drab and clinging Shelley Winters when he can have Elizabeth Taylor always in soft focus? It would be perverse. "Where are you going when you leave here?" a girl asks Brando in *The*

Wild One. "We just go," he says; and later expands this idea. "You don't go any one special place, that's cornball style. You just gotta go."

Still, the contrasts are striking. Delinquents and hoboes appear in one set of movies only to fade into sentimentality, their threatening presence swamped with reassuring reflections: they're not bad, those kids, just a little wild, a little mixed up, they'll settle down. In the musicals there are neither delinquents nor sentimentality, but brisk, exuberant assertions about how much fun there is to be had out of life. It becomes all the more intriguing, then, to watch these musicals as they fail to keep the darkening world out of their sunny perspectives, as they gradually give in to all the gloom they have tried so bravely to hold at bay.

I am thinking, as I said before, of the MGM musical, of the musical that says what it has to say in music, as distinct from a movie that has music in it. If we compare *High Society* (1955), say, with *An American in Paris*, the difference becomes very clear. *High Society* has Bing Crosby, Frank Sinatra, Louis Armstrong, and a fine score by Cole Porter. But the music, splendid as it is, has nothing to do with what the movie is about. Grace Kelly, as a frigid Brahmin beauty, has to learn to unbend and be human (*High Society* is *The Philadelphia Story*, 1940, done up with tunes). Everything in the movie tells this story, above all the very attractive presence of Grace Kelly herself, and the music just hangs around, decorative but pointless. In *An American in Paris*, on the other hand, everything that counts gets into the music. How little it matters, for example, that Gene Kelly should be a painter; how much it matters that he should sing and dance "I Got Rhythm" with a group of French children. That is not only what he is in the movie for, it is what the movie itself is about: having rhythm and all that that implies about a capacity to look on the bright, gaily colored side of things. Life, it seems, aspires to the condition of a ballet danced to a Gershwin suite.

Even the Astaire and Rogers films don't offer this degree of integration of music and meaning, and it is this so-called integral musical that fades in the fifties. John Russell Taylor, in *The Hollywood Musical*, sees the great age at MGM as running from *Cabin in the Sky* (1943) to *It's Always Fair Weather* (1955). Douglas McVay, in *The Musical Film*, sees the heyday starting a year later, with *Meet Me in St. Louis* (1944), and ending a couple of years sooner, with *The Band Wagon* (1953). Even if we allow the period to stretch all the way from *The Wizard of Oz* (1939) to *Bells Are Ringing* (1960), it still shows the astonishingly rapid rise and fall of a whole genre. "What defeated this movement in films," Russell Taylor writes,

was apparently nothing inherent, but one of those unaccountable changes of public taste, which brought about a turning-away from musicals in the cinema, unless they were pre-sold re-recreations of some theatre show that had been enjoyed.

It was nothing inherent in the musicals, certainly, and changes in taste are always to some degree unaccountable. But this change, surely, has clear echoes and parallels in many areas of American life in the fifties. What killed off the vivid musical of those years was a growing failure of music in the life outside the movies. By the mid-fifties, it was beginning to seem impossible to break into a general song and dance in America, even metaphorically, and

153

Gene Kelly's beaming face—although Kelly hadn't changed, poor fellow—was the frozen mask of confidence lost beyond all recall.

We can trace this decline in three movies; the shift in mood seems almost imperceptible from the first to the second, but almost shocking from the second to the third. The films I have in mind are *On the Town, Singin' in the Rain*, and *It's Always Fair Weather*. All three were produced by Arthur Freed, all three were written by Adolph Green and Betty Comden, all three were directed by Gene Kelly and Stanley Donen, and all three starred Kelly himself.

On the Town follows what has been a standard lineup in musicals since the thirties: the threesome. One tall, one short, and one middle-sized; one boyish, one soulful, one comic; and so on. Since it does recur so often, the lineup is obviously important. It provides a movie with a three-headed hero, with a character divided into three aspects. And it also asserts the virtues of working in a team, three as one. *On the Town*, in fact, has two threesomes, for good measure: three boys who meet three girls.

Meetings are what musicals are so often about: getting people together, getting things together. Conflicts are not only resolved, they are transfigured in music. That is the formal pattern of the dance routines of Astaire and Rogers: a set of refusals that becomes an assent. And that is also a reason why so many musicals are about putting on a show. The music marks the progression toward getting the show on the road, and finally celebrates the show itself as the end of all the quarrels that were threatening its very existence.

On the Town, then, sends out three sailors for a day in New York and ends with their return to their ship, to be followed by three other similarly disparate sailors bounding off for their own day on the town. This was a typical, musical day. The Navy met New York, boys met girls, war met peace. It goes on all the time, and New York, New York, the opening song says, is a wonderful town.

But beyond these encounters, the movie is dominated by its driving dance numbers: "New York, New York;" the title piece, in which Kelly and his pals (Frank Sinatra and Jules Munshin) dance on top of, and then down and out of the Empire State Building in a fury of glee and determination; and a routine called "Prehistoric Man," led by Ann Miller and set in the Natural History Museum. (Her father has sent her there in the hope that the study of Man will cure her of men, but it hasn't.) Everything in the movie comes to cluster around what is being urged in these songs and dances, and here I have to lapse into a clumsy transcription of what, after all, is not being said in words. There is a relentless energy in these routines; a sense that the city and the world can be taken on and beaten; there is a joy which is ready to batter on all doors. The city is acknowledged in its potential ugliness, but it can't contain or depress all this rage to possess and spend life. There is very little kindness in the movie, and not much of a feeling of happiness. But there is a frantic *will* to be happy, a conviction that you don't really have to get tired, ever. That is why it is such an exhausting movie, and exhilarating only when you have recovered your breath and think back on it.

Singin' in the Rain is calmer, a show-business movie about sound coming to Hollywood and confounding the silent stars. But there are numbers that Kelly shares first with Donald O'Connor ("Moses"), and then with O'Connor and Debbie Reynolds ("Good Mornin' ") that have much the same connotations as the fast routines in *On the Town.* An elocution lesson is turned into a crazy tap dance when Kelly and O'Connor make jazz out of the jingles they are meant to be mastering ("Moses supposes his toeses are roses, / But Moses supposes erroneously" *). A whole batch of domestic objects is rounded up and danced with. These are precisely the connections that great musicals are always making; these are just the continuities they insist on: our speech can be nudged into music, our way of walking can be edged into a dance; and the things in our house are all possible props for an improvised ballet. And it all adds up to a declaration of confidence. Two or three people tap dancing in perfect time are two or three people who are flawlessly together—and if we like to see them as aspects of a single character too, they are a person who has got himself together. Fantasies of success are being offered here, but they are not being offered as fantasies; rather as promises, chances, opportunities, indications; and they suggest not so much how to succeed as how it feels to be succeeding.

The private assertion of this is the solo rendering of the title number by Gene Kelly after he has taken Debbie Reynolds home. This is a virtuoso performance of great charm, however it sounds in the moral atmosphere of *A Clockwork Orange;* it is jaunty, tender, witty, romantic, and intimates convincingly that a man in those days really could collect his feelings with this kind of relaxed control,

* From "Moses," by Roger Edens, Betty Comden, and Adolph Green. © 1952 Metro-Goldwyn-Mayer Corporation, New York. Rights throughout the world are controlled by Robbins Music Corporation. Used by permission.

Singin' in the Rain (1952): Confidence—Gene Kelly sings (and dances) in the studio rain. From the MGM release *Singin' in the Rain*. © 1952 Loew's, Incorporated.

sing about them, and dance them out on a public street in the rain. The world, represented by a passing policeman, will think such antics are ridiculous, but it won't think they're insane. The only sequence in the movie that makes one wonder about a crack in all this confidence is a number danced and sung by O'Connor called "Make 'Em Laugh"—the demonstration of energy is far too energetic, and the film, like Hamlet's mother only with rather different sentiments, is protesting too much.

It's Always Fair Weather trots out its title as if nothing had happened, as if the state of mind represented by Gene Kelly were immortal. But the movie itself unmistakably indicates the reverse: This is not fair weather at all, and not even Kelly can sing in this rain. The music by André Previn is stricken with the same disease of the spirit that afflicts the entire movie. Here, three soldiers hit the town, but not for a spree and not to find love. They are separating now, because the war is over, and their civilian lives beckon. And Gene Kelly, instead of meeting a girl like Vera-Ellen, as in *On the Town*, gets a letter from his girl saying she has married someone else. True, he does meet Cyd Charisse, which is not bad going, and the three pals do meet again, and after some grim disagreements, do get their old friendship going again. But the opening of the movie is so elegiac, so much a retraction of every energetic premise that gets musicals off the ground, that it colors everything. When Kelly reads the letter from his girl, all three soldiers decide to get drunk, and then they dance, a routine that takes them over taxicabs and under an overpass and ends with them stomping gracelessly around on garbage-can lids. Apart from the harshness of the scene itself, something very strange has happened.

I should make it clear perhaps that I do not attribute

It's Always Fair Weather (1955): Confidence cracking—Gene Kelly skates to music, trying a little too hard to like himself. From the MGM release *It's Always Fair Weather.* © 1955 Loew's, Incorporated.

subtle, self-damaging intentions to the writers or the directors here—I think they just wanted to make a musical and this is the way it turned out. But the movie as we have it speaks unequivocally: In the world as it is, in order to sing and dance you have to be drunk. One could hardly be further from the world of Fred Astaire, or even from the world of Gene Kelly's earlier movies.

The same failing vision is confirmed later in the movie when Dan Dailey, listening to his business colleagues talk, picks up the rhythm of a march and starts to move to it. He does, in short, exactly what Kelly and O'Connor do in their elocution lesson in *Singin' in the Rain:* finds rhythm in regularity, music in noise. Only here it is not fun but a sort of anxiety: he is on the edge of a breakdown. When he finally does get a dance number out of these same rhythms, he is, again, drunk, and the dance is represented, not as something emerging from ordinary life, but as a violent onslaught on a stifling, unmusical world, a drastic, liberating Marx Brothers romp—a revolt against normality, not a transfiguration of it.

In two instances the film finds its way back to the old musical vein: the first, a number that Cyd Charisse does with a gang of bruisers at a gymnasium ("Baby, You Knock Me Out"), where some of that earlier willingness to face all futures seems still alive; the second, a dazzling variation on his "Singin' in the Rain" solo by Gene Kelly, wearing the same suit and hat, but in fair weather and with an even wider grin and on roller skates. The skates serve to draw out the dance, to elongate and parody the whole style developed by Astaire and Kelly, so that it becomes a slightly alarming affair of excessive glides and tilts and some very fancy dueling with the law of gravity and the tempo of the music. It is a brilliant number—in part, homage to Chaplin swirling around a department store on skates in *Modern Times,* and to Astaire and Rogers dancing on skates in *Shall We Dance*—and no musical with a tour de force like this in it is really dead. Even so, the sense of echoes from other movies, and the flaunted technical virtuosity create the mood of an implicit farewell, a crowning caricature.

There is one moment in *It's Always Fair Weather* where almost all of this decline and disintegration comes across at once. There are lots of movies about movies, of course—*Singin' in the Rain* is one—but I can think of no other scene which says quite so painfully and so unforgettably what it means to make a movie that is only a movie, nothing more. The three old war buddies have separated, and each is alone and disappointed with the others and with himself. But to us, they are together in three distinct sections of a split screen, dancing in time to the same music. That is, they are alone in the plot but together in the film image and in the choreography; lost in their lives but found in the physical confines of the movie. Later the plot brings them together again, but never convincingly, and the movie ends in a brawl which is something less than uplifting. There is simply nothing in the movie to cancel this central paradox and confession: These are people bound to each other by an optical illusion, synchronized in a trick; and beyond them we can glimpse a whole society in which analogues for fancy camerawork pretend to cement what has long ago come asunder.

All right, it's no news to anyone that Americans in the fifties were not as happy as they pretended to be. When Eisenhower was ill in 1955, the stock market took its steepest drop since 1929, and one can well understand how a little despair might creep into a film like *It's Always Fair Weather*. The very title sounds like Eisenhower's motto. Perhaps my exploration of these fading musicals is just another spectacular triumph for hindsight.

I think it is, in part. But then hindsight *is* a form of sight, and I think we need to pay attention to it now and again. If you see *Picnic*, now, for example, you are likely to be struck by the persistent, insidious hysteria which seems to haunt this romantically photographed episode in the national heartland. The anxiety of Kim Novak's mother to marry her off to the local rich lad seems frenzied, rather than mildly and mistakenly ambitious (which is how it used to seem). The sexual distress of Rosalind Russell, stranded in her starved and aging provincial life as a schoolteacher, verges on panic, and the scene in which she clings so desperately to William Holden that she tears his shirt off almost tilts the movie into uncontrollable melodrama. And this America, this place that seemed so pastoral on earlier viewings of the film, takes on the quality of incipient nightmare. Not because the director, Joshua Logan, shot the movie as nightmare, and not because anyone saw it as nightmare in 1955 or long after; but because now, in the mid-seventies, the lineaments of nightmare stand out in disturbing clarity.

It is not a question of our being right now and wrong then—or right then and wrong now. We were right both times—and wrong both times, no doubt, to a degree: nobody's perfect, as Joe E. Brown says to Jack Lemmon at the end of *Some Like It Hot*. It is a question of our being able to see, for once, how a change in our mood takes shape. The frustrated spinster who seemed merely one of the casualties of wholesome, ordinary, heterosexual, monogamous American life in the fifties, a figure of fun with a faint edge of pain to her, now seems an emblem of a loneliness that has itself become ordinary.

And the loneliness was there in the fifties, in *Picnic*. It was muffled by the other emphasis we chose to give to the film, but we did see its hopeless and frantic gestures, we did hear its angry and embittered words, and this is precisely the function I am proposing for popular movies. They permit us to look without looking at things we can neither face fully nor entirely disavow. We don't usually notice this function, but then it is because we don't notice—because the distress lurking in *Picnic* and *It's Always Fair Weather* merely lurks and never pounces—that these movies work so well as myths. When we see them as myths, it's too late, because we are already living among new myths we have yet to recognize.

"I like myself." The line has a wishful sound. Once you start singing that you're surely in trouble, and you begin to need a president like Eisenhower, that worried icon of American self-satisfaction. But what about the earlier musicals, the ones where American confidence was still in genuine full swing, were there no doubts in them? Not really. The confidence was very impressive, and that is why it seems so unreal now, seen from our shaky times. Or rather there was one doubt, and it has to do with the quality of Gene Kelly's screen personality; it is contained in Kelly's style in the way that so many American dreams of loneliness came to congregate in Bogart's face.

For Kelly was always trying too hard. If the musical characteristically gets things together, and if Fred Astaire always got them together by grace and nonchalant artistry, then Kelly was the man for the more diffident and superstitious among us, for all those of us who never can quite believe in their good fortune, and for whom Astaire's style seems wonderful but inaccessible, remote in its very unobtrusiveness. You can worry, that is, about a confidence you no longer have, and that is what Americans came to do in the course of the fifties. But you can also worry about a confidence you really possess, and this, it seems to me, is Kelly's gift: He suggests fantastic skill edged with uncertainty. He's got things together but his achievement seems too precarious for him to be happy. He can't rest. He is a portrait of America before the plague of locusts which came in the shape of Hiss, Korea, the Rosenbergs, McCarthy, and the rest, and that is why he seems to belong to the day before yesterday, the day before Eisenhower. But part of his appeal is a touch of strain and even faint fear, an air of scenting locusts on the wind, not because he or anyone foresaw what would happen to America in the fifties, and not because his confidence was anything but real, but simply because all good things come to an end, and some of us do worry when we are doing well. And we are right to worry. If we are not Fred Astaire, we won't last forever. Whatever your skill, and however doggedly you smile and you dance and you like yourself, it isn't really always fair weather anywhere in the world, and singing in the rain, if it becomes a habit, can sound very much like whistling in the dark.

VIII

Shake the Superflux

Cecil B. De Mille,
Much against his will,
Was persuaded to keep Moses
Out of the Wars of the Roses.

Anonymous

. . . Take physic, pomp,
Expose thyself to feel what wretches feel,
That thou mayst shake the superflux to them
And show the heavens more just.

Shakespeare,
King Lear

THE *Autobiography* of Cecil B. De Mille, that master of cinematic overstatement, is full of casual, quiet lines, small-scale remarks whose grandiose implications come clear only some moments after you have read them: "The greatest single problem in *The Ten Commandments* (1956) was the Voice of God. . . ." De Mille also modestly admitted that "directing scenes in which 8,000 people take

part at one time is never easy. . . ." Setting up the City of
the Pharaohs in modern Egypt was, he tells us, a "gigantic
task," which the reader will appreciate, "if he has ever had
any experience of building, equipping, and peopling a city
in a foreign country." I don't think De Mille means to
write as if he expected Alexander the Great to be his only
reader. He likes to describe his firm way with recalcitrant
lions and elephants, and his favorite simile for the big
production is military:

> I have sometimes compared a producer to a commanding gen-
> eral, who must see that all the units of his armies, with all their
> distinct functions in the coming battle, are ready to strike simul-
> taneously on the target date.

Of course De Mille is merely adopting with compla-
cency a view of himself (and other producers and directors) that usually comes in less flattering forms. Harry
Cohn was often said to run Columbia Pictures like a concentration camp, and Philip French reminds us that the
movie moguls, in his book of that title, were very keen on
Napoleon, "that hero of small men and megalomaniacs."
But De Mille's remarks take on a special interest when we
remember that in the fifties and early sixties Hollywood
went over to De Mille in a big way, fell for the epic spectacle as the promised salvation of the industry, so that
Selznick, for example, in 1953, found himself cautioning
L. B. Mayer, who was contemplating a show called *Joseph
and His Brethren*, loosely stemming from Thomas Mann,
that "there has appeared only one Cecil B. De Mille"
and that "nothing is more appalling than second-rate
De Mille."

Very soon nothing was more frequent, either. De

Mille's own *Samson and Delilah* (1949) had been sold to very
skeptical backers by means of cheesecake portraits of Victor Mature and Hedy Lamarr, sweating and sultry, respectively. But then *Quo Vadis?* (1951) did well; *The Robe*
(1953) seemed to prove that the ancient world had a certain pull at the box office; by 1956, De Mille had remade
his earlier *Ten Commandments* (1923), which merely had a
biblical prologue, into a vast biblical spread in its own
right; and by 1959, William Wyler had remade the old
Ben-Hur into possibly the best of all these late Hollywood
blossoms of excess. By the time the ill-starred production
of *Cleopatra* (released in 1963) was under way, the vogue of
the epic was so strongly established that it could provoke
its own epic diasters. There had been *David and Bathsheba*
(1952), *The Egyptian* (1954), *Land of the Pharaohs* (1955),
Alexander the Great (1956), *Spartacus* (1960), *King of
Kings* (1961), and *Barabbas* (1962). Yet to come were *Sodom
and Gomorrah* (1963), *The Fall of the Roman Empire* (1964),
The Greatest Story Ever Told (1965), and *The Bible* (1966). It
may not have been the best of times or the worst of times,
but it was certainly one of the biggest of times in the
movies.

Size was the thing, what Selznick (who should know)
called "the big feel." Indeed, Selznick's letter to Mayer
belongs very clearly to the universe of De Mille's *Autobiography*, even to the universe of many of De Mille's films.
The style is very different, for Selznick is dogged and
fussy where De Mille is offhand and lordly, but what is
said is remarkably similar. Both men assume that what
God (for De Mille) and posterity (for Selznick) want above
all else from the human race is a vast, well-intentioned,
high-toned, commercially successful movie. "I am all too

aware that you want a big show," Selznick writes to Mayer about *Joseph and His Brethren* (I quote from Rudy Behlmer's *Memo from David O. Selznick*):

You have working for you that greatest of all showmanship combinations—sex and religion. You have father love, mother love, brother love; you have lust and sentiment; you have a faithful husband and you have an unfaithful wife; you have complete blueprints for every conceivable production value, including spectacle, exterior scenes of great beauty, interiors of great pomp and circumstance, magnificent costumes, daring and revealing costumes, boudoir scenes, royalty and panoply, family life—indeed the whole catalog of elements of mass appeal. . . . Put them all together even in sloppy fashion, give them a good production, fairly good actors, fairly good direction, Technicolor or its equivalent, and good exploitation, and Louis B. Mayer will not fail to have a big-grossing, a very big-grossing film. *But* add to these the ultimate in quality and integrity of approach, add to them idealism worthy of a Thomas Mann, and *there* will be a motion picture to be remembered for generations. . . .

Something like Selznick's *Gone With The Wind*, in short. (*Joseph and His Brethren* was never made.) The accepted explanation of Hollywood's fever of epics in the fifties and sixties is that epics provided an answer to television, for they offered all the color and crowds and overwhelming visual effects that you couldn't get on the small (and then black-and-white) screen: chariot races, the burning of Rome, the dividing of the Red Sea, and the crucifixion, complete with attendant miracles and darkness creeping across the stereoscopic face of the land. This ought to have made the epics a kind of celebration of pure cinema, an expression of the cinema as self-advertisement, a demonstration of what the medium could do. But by a slight and characteristic Hollywood slip, the part was taken somehow for the whole, and the epics became demonstrations of what a *studio* could do; they were the last grand flings of those factories of illusion.

A certain style of cinema—De Mille's, roughly—thus comes to stand for the American cinema itself, as if the cure for defecting audiences and closing picture houses were to put all your eggs in one basket; in the largest basket you could find. (Between 1951 and 1958 the weekly moviegoing public in America fell from 90 million to 42 million; between 1946 and 1959 the number of cinemas in America—excluding drive-ins—fell from 20,000 to 11,000). The fight against television was conceived as a duel of screens, as a matter of size of image, but it quickly became a matter of size of budget. The amount of money spent on a film was part of what helped to sell the film— on the principle, presumably, that anything that had cost that much had to be good, and also if it cost that much, we were invited to think, just imagine how much it will make. A projection of fabulous success for the movie be‑ comes part of the movie's story before it even reaches the cinema. To be sure, this was always a Hollywood princi‑ ple, but the epics consecrated it and interiorized it, so to speak, as if it were the only principle the industry had left. The expense of an epic is not only an item in an advertis‑ ing campaign, it is an aspect of the movie as you see it. Only epics, I think, insist on our thinking so much about money while we are in the cinema. Every gesture, every set piece bespeaks fantastic excess: There is more of every‑ thing, and especially there are more extras drawing what we all think of (erroneously) as magnificent daily pay, than even an excessive movie could possibly need. We sit there and brood about (and vaguely exult in) the sheer extrava‑ gance of setting up the Exodus from Egypt, say, in this exorbitant way, as an innumerable army of men, women, children, animals, carts, and wagons trundle out toward Canaan. De Mille's own description of the shooting of this scene in *The Ten Commandments* has all the self-consciousness and self-celebration that the scene itself has in the film. What is happening here is something like the reverse of mimesis. This is not an imitation of life but a complete replacement of life by a life-size simulacrum: A full-scale model of the Exodus makes the real Exodus seem pale by comparison. The real Exodus, after all, was not conceived and executed by a single movie producer (unless we think of God in that role) solely as a form of mass entertainment:

It was a warm day. Again and again the crowd of extras trudged before the camera, packed together, laden down with their babies and their household goods, jostled not only by each other but by water buffalo, wagons, and the whole surge of a nation on the move.

Directing scenes in which 8,000 people take part at one time is never easy.

I don't mean to suggest that we all think technically about such scenes as we see them, merely that even the most innocent and credulous among us have a sense of the Exodus in *The Ten Commandments* (and big scenes in many other epics) as technical achievements and not just as significant moments in a story being told to us. Even as we are stirred by the spectacle (and it *is* stirring), we are thinking of it as a triumph of lavish expenditure and of human engineering. The note of conspicuous production, to use Adorno and Horkheimer's adaptation of a phrase from Veblen, is never far from any of these movies, and we can follow an odd and compelling train of logic in them: Size means a big screen, and a big screen has to be

The Ten Commandments (1956): Nothing succeeds like excess—
C. B. De Mille lets his people go. © 1956 Paramount Pictures
Corporation.

filled with big things, like cities being built and burned, like well-attended Roman circuses, like nations on the move; and all this means ingenuity and authority and money, and ingenuity, authority, and money quickly become the almost overt subject of these films.

Vestiges of all this remain in Hollywood, in the shape of the preoccupation with the "action" that Joan Didion described so well in an article in *The New York Review of Books*. (March 22, 1973). Didion's movie folk race around waving large checks, as if *inventing* movies—putting movie packages together—were what movies are all about. Even the money involved, Didion suggests, is less "real" money than a totem of the action in progress. "The action itself is the art form, and is described in aesthetic terms." The piece concludes with an account of a film that didn't get made. Everyone has regrets, but only faint ones:

> It had been a very creative deal and they had run with it as far as they could run and they had had some fun and now the fun was over, as it would also have been had they made the picture.

Such people are the true, if febrile, heirs of the old moguls, scattered remnants of romantic capitalism. For that is what the old Hollywood was—or rather that was what Hollywood meant to many Americans, Fitzgerald included. It was pirate's capitalism, risky, swashbuckling adventure on the Fiscal Main, it was capitalism with its ancient panache intact, and the producer, in the old mythology, was its garish hero and emblem: the author of all the action. In the movies themselves, though, the producer's role as horrid, compelling monster (or alternatively, as dynamic, all-purpose genius, like Fitzgerald's Monroe Stahr, modeled on Irving Thalberg) came to be taken by the epic: the embodiment of feckless, coarse, heroic, *American* extravagance: still the first thought in many people's minds when Hollywood is mentioned.

When Hollywood speaks of itself as an industry, Adorno and Horkheimer maintain, the truth is being used as an ideology. The epics were the ideology of the ideology. They were Hollywood's own version of *The Last Tycoon:* flights, as Fitzgerald said of his novel, into "a lavish, romantic past that perhaps will not come again into our time." Selznick, speaking to Ben Hecht, compared Hollywood to Egypt ("full of crumbled pyramids"), but he was not making a casual analogy—or if he was, he spoke truer than he thought. For Hollywood was Egypt, and Rome, and Jerusalem. The ancient world of the epics was a huge, many-faceted metaphor for Hollywood itself, because even when shot on location or in studios in Italy and Spain, these movies are always *about* the creation of such a world in a movie, about Hollywood's capacity to duplicate old splendors, to bring Egypt and Rome to the screen, as the old phrase had it. They are about the achievements of De Mille as a general, about the crowds he managed to mobilize and control, and about the lions and elephants he bullied into behaving properly for the camera. The hero of *The Ten Commandments* is not Moses, but De Mille himself, who set up the whole show, the voice of God and the burning bush and the miracles in Egypt included. And the hero of *Ben-Hur* is not Ben-Hur, who only won the chariot race, but William Wyler, the director, the man responsible for providing the chariot race for us.

Whatever reasons led Hollywood to its fifties and sixties epics, made both at home and abroad (a Dino de Laurentiis production, said a smug executive at Paramount, is a Hollywood team on location in Rome); whatever motives of self-defense and self-advertisement; whatever pangs of nostalgia for a great age already gone, for movie dynasties smitten by the antitrust laws much as ancient Rome was beaten down by the barbarians, the epic quickly outgrew its origins and became a genre in its own right. The crowds and the set pieces, displayed, no doubt, in the first place to threaten television and signal vast expenditure, became elements in an ongoing story, articulations of a genuine American myth: the myth of excess, the myth that suggests, in many places and in many forms, that only those things that are too big are big enough for American appetites, and that only too much is really sufficient.

There is a certain puzzle about the limits of the epic as a genre. It seems, for example, that most films set in the ancient world turn out to be epics. On the other hand, a number of movies not set in the ancient world, like *El Cid* (1961), and *Khartoum* (1966), and *Lawrence of Arabia* (1962), also clearly belong. I am inclined to believe that the presence of Charlton Heston alone, apart from any other factors, is almost enough to turn any movie into an epic; but then his presence doesn't do anything along this line for *The War Lord* (1965). An epic is not just any historical film, and not just an expensive film, and not just a *big* film, at least in some senses of the word big. *Cleopatra*, for example, is a failed epic and a poor movie; but George Stevens's *Giant* is a fairly good movie that fails to be an epic. It is long, ambitious, spectacular, and an attempt to make Texas into an epic theme, but it succeeds only in making Texas a sprawling backdrop to a family saga, a sort of Whiteoaks amid the oil rigs and the cattle.

The basic elements of the epic seem to run from relatively minor ones like the music (preferably by Miklos Rozsa or Elmer Bernstein, always a martial, pompous affair, with lots of organs and trumpets, a mixture of Elgar, Episcopalian hymns, and Handel, alternating with soulful, exotic-sounding slow movements for the love scenes, variations on the tunes we usually associate with snake charming) to relatively major ones like certain sturdy, straight-faced acting styles to absolutely essential elements like the big scenes (the orgy, the ceremonial entry into the city, the great battle, the individual combat, and where possible, a miracle or two) and the big, earthshaking themes.

This last item is a good clue to what we are looking for. What is wrong with *Giant* is that we don't feel world history is being made in that story. What is wrong with *Cleopatra* (among other things) is that its private lives don't link up in any forceful way with its imperial subject, so that we merely see confused people making a mess of things on the margins of history. There is no sense of individuals entangled in momentous doings, as Moses is in *The Ten Commandments;* or subtly tied to the religious big time, as Ben-Hur is in *Ben-Hur,* meeting Christ during the early days of His ministry, catching a piece of the Sermon on the Mount, and dropping in on the crucifixion; or being present right at the start of things, as Robert Taylor and Deborah Kerr are in *Quo Vadis?,* their love blossoming out into the kingdom without end of Christianity. Mankiewicz tries for this effect in *Cleopatra,* at least intermittently, and there is a fair amount of lofty dialogue in the movie. "The world," Elizabeth Taylor says to Rex Harrison as Caesar, "except for you, is filled with little men." "Suddenly," Richard Burton says after Harrison's death, "I have the pieces of a broken world to pick up." There is a big theme threaded through the film, the theme of Alexander's old ambition of uniting east and west, Egypt and Rome, into one gigantic empire. But this grandiose vision doesn't seem to ignite any epic energy in the movie, remains oddly formal, lifeless, literary; and it is in any case a failed vision, whereas epics thrive on historical success—especially the success of small persecuted groups, like the Jews in Egypt and the Christians in Rome, people who have God on their side, so that we see all their present sufferings and setbacks through the glass of our secure knowledge of their spectacular future triumph. Antony and Cleopatra don't triumph, and the two major set pieces in the film, Cleopatra's entry into Rome and the battle of Actium, set the genre and the story at each other's throats. These demonstrations of excess and technical virtuosity, these conspicuous productions ("Nothing like this has come into Rome since Romulus and Remus," Burton says as Cleopatra checks in with her train of tall Nubians, various animals, numerous dancing girls and a vast sphinx) all lack just that exuberance which De Mille always gave to such scenes, and which is what they are ultimately about. The great sea battle is a great sea fiasco—it is the battle of Actium, after all, and apart from the technical poverty of its execution, it is where Antony turns around and runs. It isn't necessary that the hero should win all his big battles, even in an epic, but it certainly is desirable that he should stay and fight. *Cleopatra* has all the ingredients of a great elegy, a Hollywood swan song, and hardly any of the elements of an epic, and while the immense snags and difficulties encountered in the course of production must have left a heavy mark on the mood of the finished film, it is hard to see it as anything other than a perverse project, the fruit of an odd misunderstanding of the essential rules of the game it chose to play. The epic, if it meant anything, meant extravagant victory against all odds: It meant winning the chariot race and escaping Pharaoh's swiftly pursuing wrath; it meant wrestling successfully with a bull (*Quo Vadis?*), defeating the formidable Jack Palance in the arena (*Barabbas*). In the contexts of these triumphs, the movies' own engineering feats made perfect, harmonious sense, the whole show became a celebration of magnificent, improbable conquest. The best Mankiewicz could do in *Cleopatra* was a stately gloom.

The favorite historical moments of the epics—the rise of Christianity, adventures from the Old Testament—are something like hyperbolic equivalents of literary masterpieces, or of hot contemporary literary properties. They are *The Godfather*'s godfather, and the title of *The Greatest Story Ever Told* hides no secrets. If you film *War and Peace*, you are filming a book some people have read and many people feel they ought to have read. But if you film Moses receiving the Law, you are filming a classic not of literature, but of culture itself. You are giving a face to a figure everyone knows, a landscape to his life. De Mille liked to insist on how much Charlton Heston as Moses resembled Michelangelo's rendering of him, but that is hardly the point. The point is not that Heston looks like an accepted and well-known version of Moses, but that Moses now, for generations of people all over the world, looks like Charlton Heston.

Not everyone can make a pilgrimage to Sinai, De Mille wrote, so we brought Sinai to everyone on film. "One thought," De Mille said, ran through the thousands of letters he had received about *The Ten Commandments*: "This picture has made God real to me." Having to wait for God to speak in the movies may suggest a certain poverty of imagination (not to mention a dire want of faith), but the letters respond perfectly to what seems to be the central ambition of the epic as a genre, which is simply to do the biggest thing there is to do. Olivier filmed Shakespeare, but De Mille filmed God. The epic constantly aspires to be the greatest telling ever of the greatest story ever told.

It is tempting to set up a typology of big scenes in Hollywood epics, linking the cheering, respectful crowd at the triumphal entry into the city to the roaring bloodthirsty crowd in the arena; tying in the almost inevitable military victories with the calamitously recurring acts of God. But I think I'll resist the temptation. What is important is the appearance of all these scenes in movie after movie: gladiatorial combat, march of triumph, battle, miracle, orgy. When Anthony Mann's *Fall of the Roman Empire*, after much talk of gladiators and circuses, has Stephen Boyd and Christopher Plummer meet for their final fight with gladiatorial weapons, but not in a circus, the abstention seems almost ascetic, a quirky touch of originality, the signature of a movie wanting to be different. But I have scarcely mentioned what is perhaps the most interesting of all the set scenes in the epic: the great crash. Rome burns in *Quo Vadis?* and *Barabbas;* there is a mine disaster in *Barabbas* for good measure; Gaza crumbles around Samson's ears in *Samson and Delilah;* there is a wild and destructive storm in *Ben-Hur;* the earth opens to receive sinners in *The Ten Commandments.* Doom and apocalypse lurk around these optimistic movies, tokens of catastrophe surround these celebrations of success.

But more importantly, the idea of waste in these movies receives its fullest expression here. Here are costly sets, carefully built constructions going up in smoke, or toppling down in ruins, the very feats of engineering we have

Samson and Delilah (1949): The great crash—catastrophe in Gaza.
© 1949 Paramount Pictures, Inc.

just been admiring are now thrown away. This is visible expense, like the crowds of extras, only more startling. This is money being burned. We may find out, if we inquire that the blazing sets are not the sets we have just seen but leftovers from other movies given false fronts, as was the case for the lurid burning of Atlanta in *Gone With The Wind*. But the effect in the film remains. *Something* is being consumed before our eyes, and the historical Rome was at least lived in for a while before it went under. Here is an elaborate imitation of Rome which is inhabited only for a couple of big scenes before the flames take over; a Rome built, in effect, in order to be burned. The camera can't lie in this respect: the unmistakable work of human hands collapses into genuine ashes or genuine dust.

This is shaking the superflux indeed, only the meaning of the gesture is more or less the reverse of what King Lear appears to have had in mind. Excess is not being shaken out to others, but just shaken out: It is pure excess, a ritual expression of lack of need. There are complicated, pragmatic arguments in favor of a show of expense, of course: if you're spending that much, you must have a lot more; and perhaps it is only by spending so much that you can make any real money these days in the movies. Having all that cash to throw away is a sign of (apparent) financial health. But actually throwing it away is a sign of moral health, a sign that you are not hampered by your riches, and it is the throwing away that we see in the movies, the amazing prodigality.

There is a hidden credo here, it seems to me, a nagging suspicion that money is really supposed to be thrown away, to be burned, like Rome or a costly set, like Atlanta; to be wasted. America is often seen as a parsimonious place, and much is made of its thrifty, practical traditions. Yet waste strikes me as a far more impressive feature of American life. I don't mean casual, careless waste. I mean planned prodigality, spectacular waste, waste as a way of life: glass skyscrapers and cars that give you seven miles to the gallon of gasoline.

I don't think this is a reaction against a past of puritan prescriptions. It is rather the oblique expression of a faith. Here is God's plenty, or what was later known as technological abundance, and to save money or gasoline or energy is to doubt the profusion of God's gifts or the reliability of his covenant with America. Conspicuous consumption is no longer snobbery and invidious display but merely, as C. Wright Mills said, the mark of a high standard of living. What you throw away is the measure of your splendor, as Veblen suggested; and then having thrown it away you are free of it. The raw, materialistic American culture of this century seems curiously unworldly when compared to the old New England theocracy. For the Puritans, worldly goods were a token of God's blessing, a proof that you were on the right track. For many modern Americans worldly goods are so abundant that it becomes a form of scandal to want to hang on to any of them for very long. And they are a hindrance anyway. They tie you down when you want to be up and moving. Money is *meant* to be burned.

The epics thus involved Hollywood in what must have been one of the oddest gambling situations ever. They were throwing a lot of money out in the hope of getting a lot of money back: nothing odd about that. But consider the idea that grand visions of waste are a good investment. You could make money, it seemed, by suggesting that money was for burning. Well, until *Cleopatra* you could.

As soon as things go wrong, the happy prodigal in all of

us shrinks and hides, and the skulking puritan steps out. The pomp and splendor of *Ben-Hur*, the extravagances of De Mille, were large, liberating gestures, forms of taking no thought for the morrow. They assumed, though, contrary to the implications of the biblical precept, that the morrow really needed no thought, because it was taking care of itself very nicely already. The moment the morrow really needs some thought, we feel it ought to get it. When epic expense comes off (that is, turns out to be economically sound) we think it's heroic. When it fails (that is, when it is real, unredeemed expense) we think it's irresponsible. There's no success like failure, as Bob Dylan sang, and failure's no success at all. We don't really like waste. But then we don't like being careful either, and this is what the myth of excess is about. This is why a good commercial epic is so appealing. Here is gargantuan waste that makes big money. What could be finer? What could be more perfectly in the American grain?

Actors and actresses recur from epic to epic with enough frequency to suggest a repertory company on a sort of biblical tour. It is true that Hollywood in any case, as Stanley Cavell says, is or was the nation's one true stock company. The number of stars was never infinite, and performers' contracts often tied them up for a whole series of movies. Perhaps one notices the recurrence of personnel less in modern-dress films, or just writes it off as typecasting, or as what actors need to acquire and develop a screen personality. Still, the effect is striking in epics. Here are familiar faces and figures rigged up again and again in strange costumes, as if to attend a revolving fancy dress ball. Jean Simmons appears in *The Robe* and *Spartacus;* Richard Burton appears in *The Robe, Alexander the Great* and *Cleopatra;* Stephen Boyd appears in *Ben-Hur* and *The Fall of the Roman Empire;* Sophia Loren in *The Fall of the Roman Empire* and *El Cid.* Charlton Heston is Moses in *The Ten Commandments,* Ben-Hur in *Ben-Hur,* the Cid in *El Cid,* John the Baptist in *The Greatest Story Ever Told* and General Gordon in *Khartoum.* Finlay Currie, who plays St. Peter in *Quo Vadis* and one of the three Magi in *Ben-Hur,* shows up in *The Fall of the Roman Empire* as a senator, making exactly the same sort of holy speech that he made in the other two movies. At the obligatory party/orgy in *Ben-Hur* the girl hanging on Heston's arm for a moment is Eunice Gayson, the slave-girl who was in love with Leo Genn in *Quo Vadis.* It is, as they say, a small world, however big the show. I don't want to insist too much on this feature of the epics, merely to point out that it does reinforce the reflective, self-regarding quality in these films, the sense of the studio barely hidden in Egypt or Rome.

But I do want to insist on another aspect of the casting of these movies, and that is the distribution of American and English actors in them. The girls, for example, frequently devout and gentle Christians in a rough pagan world, are usually English: Jean Simmons, Deborah Kerr, Claire Bloom. The heroes are American: Robert Taylor, Kirk Douglas, Charlton Heston, Stephen Boyd. But then these are military men, or slaves, or Jews, and the *other* men, the ruling class, are again almost invariably English: Peter Ustinov, Alec Guinness, Laurence Olivier, Christopher Plummer. I don't mean to suggest, of course, that this pattern is intentional, merely that it reveals some interesting assumptions, since it clearly hints at a famous old transatlantic story: The English have manners and purity while the Americans have life; the decadent English, like the rotten Romans they so often portray, have a wonderful past while the energetic Americans, like the Christians and Jews in these stories, are promised a fabulous tomorrow. Still, I wouldn't harp on this if it were not that a highly simplified rendering of the American Revolution is a favorite source for the plots of these movies; and that American movies, on this showing, are only imperfectly on the side of America. Or to put that more strongly: that American movies, while they obviously believe in America in principle, are in practice almost passionate partisans of George III.

The favorite epic story, as I have suggested, concerns a persecuted group secretly supported by God: Jews, Christians, and occasionally slaves. Their oppressors are Egyptians, Romans, patricians. It is the colonies against the mean mother country. Let me be clear. I am not attributing sneaky allegorical motives to the makers of these movies, I am just saying that there aren't all that many models for a big confrontation between a powerful (but doomed) tyrant and a virtuous victim whose virtue, in the end, will reap rich historical rewards. This is the encounter that takes place again and again in epics, and it seems natural that American moviemakers should, no doubt unconsciously, fall back on a popular version of their country's birth.

All these stories invite our sympathy for the oppressed, of course—all the more so because we know that by generously backing these losers we shall find we have backed winners in the end. But then the movies, themselves, as costly studio productions, plainly take the other side.

They root for George III against the founding fathers, they are all for tyranny and Rome, more imperialist than the emperor. The great scenes in these films, the reasons for our being in the cinema at all—the orgies, the triumphs, the gladiatorial games—all belong to the oppressors. The palaces, the costumes, the pomp—"every conceivable production value," as Selznick said—are all theirs. It is the Romans who provide the circuses, who give us a Rome to be gaudily burned. It is Nero and the Pharaohs who throw the parties with all the dancing girls (no great bonus this, though, since Hollywood seemed mysteriously to have got stuck with Farouk or Aly Khan for its idea of what a despot does with his spare time). An epic on the subject of Robin Hood is unthinkable, because it would fawn so on the Sheriff of Nottingham. Certainly Sinai and the desert are impressive in *The Ten Commandments*, but they are fighting against the genre rather than riding with it. De Mille only *photographed* them, whereas he actually built and peopled the City of the Pharaohs, and this is where George III, so to speak, comes into his own in the movies.

We have returned to De Mille's notion of the producer as a general, except that we are now looking at it from the other side. For the epic as a genre is terrified of mobs, frightened by the presence in the story of those extras it delights in calling on to the set. Hollywood generally has always disliked the idea of the crowd, and even very liberal movies tend to sprout illiberal sentiments when large numbers of people are concerned. But only in the epic, perhaps, is the mob so unavoidably present on the screen, swarming about like a lot of *sans-culottes* on their way to the Bastille. The cast of thousands which requires a general to command it, the nation on the move, as De Mille says, looks like a potential peasants' revolt if you're feeling tired, and the studio's success in keeping things under control throws curious shadows into the film itself, in the shape of snatches of dialogue and twists of action that hint at what happens when you lose control of the *canaille*.

Thus the Children of Israel, in *The Ten Commandments*, are a curiously fickle lot, considering their well-known patience during 400 years of suffering. They are ready to stone Moses when he fails to liberate them instantly just by asking Pharaoh to let his people go. No sooner have they been saved by a miracle at the Red Sea than they get restless at Moses' absence on the mountain (he's picking up the Ten Commandments), and egged on by Edward G. Robinson, secede to worship the Golden Calf and go in for all kinds of riotous living. Jesse L. Lasky, Jr., in his *Whatever Happened to Hollywood?*, speaks of this as "the most difficult moment in the script," redeemed in the movie by Robinson's acting. Lasky blames it all on the Bible. Admittedly the Bible is often slack about verisimilitude, but it does take seventeen chapters of *Exodus* to get us from the Red Sea to the Golden Calf, where De Mille (or his writers) allow us only five minutes or less. De Mille was probably in a hurry by this stage of the filming. He was ill, and may have crowded things together in order to get them done. But the effect of the crowding—the suggestion of the total untrustworthiness of people as a mass—can be found in epics that were presumably not hurriedly finished. The crowd in *Barabbas*, for example, is easily persuaded to stone a girl to death, and later, at the circus, is enraged because a Christian gladiator decently refuses to kill his defeated enemy. The crowd at the circus in all these movies is always hungry for blood, as if it were some sort of human answer to the famished lions; and when Rex Harrison as Caesar thinks of his epilepsy, he says, "I shall tumble down before the mob, and make them laugh. And they will tear me to pieces."

There is an odd moment at the end of *The Ten Commandments*, which pulls a great deal of all this together. Charlton Heston as Moses takes leave of his family and sets off up the mountain to die. He steps on to a large rock, and turns to wave goodbye, raising his hand in salute. The shot is too long for comfort: not long enough to afford a sweeping epic conclusion, a tiny human figure on a landscape, about to vanish into the vastness of God; not close enough to insist on the human ending here, on Moses the man and husband and father leaving his individual life. The shot is longer than a medium shot, that is, but shorter than a proper long shot, and at this awkward distance a man raising his hand looks just like the Statue of Liberty seen across New York Bay. The effect may be accidental, but I don't think I'm hallucinating it. If it's not accidental, of course, it's probably still not entirely intentional, and I wouldn't like to guess whose unconscious is speaking in that frame. Nevertheless, the icon is there, eloquent and perfectly suited to the real theme of the movie: liberty as a slightly forbidding, only rhetorically and theoretically attractive ideal; a statue rather than a practice. The Children of Israel exchange the tyranny of men, as De Mille puts it in a spoken prologue to the film, for what looks like the tyranny of God, although De Mille doesn't quite say that. What he piously says in his *Autobiography* is that the "Law of God is the essential bedrock of human freedom"; but what this means in the movie is that those hapless and fickle Jews have escaped human bondage only to run into those ten harsh commandments. This is the sort of freedom that means you have to do just as you're told, especially if there are a lot of you. The Statue of Liberty beckons in Moses' last gesture, welcomes us all to a paradoxical America, the democratic haven of people who don't like the people.

IX
The Sense of the Past

> Another hour passed. Dreams hung in
> fragments at the far end of the room,
> suffered analysis, passed—to be dreamed
> in crowds, or else discarded.
>
> F. Scott Fitzgerald,
> *The Last Tycoon*

FILMS in our century serve one of the purposes that
novels and magazines have always served. They are dos-
siers of instruction on our social life, handbooks of better
behavior—even when better sometimes means worse, as
when Marlon Brando taught a whole generation how to be
rude. People watch movies, or used to, in the way others
read fiction, the way millions read *Elle* and *Woman's Day*
and *Woman's Own* and *Playboy*, and even *The New Yorker*:
as guides to style. Movies incessantly provide us with
manners, with ways of talking and dressing and standing
and slouching about. When Clark Gable appeared on the

screen without an undershirt, half of male America threw its undershirt away, and a national industry was (so to speak) up in arms.

But all this, widespread and significant and fascinating as it is, is a question of surfaces, and the most pervasive effects of movies arise, I think, not through an imitation of what movies show but through an acquiescence in the shapes they give to experience. I don't mean we always trust what the movies say. I mean we accept the terms and horizons of their stories—a story in this sense being not merely a plot, but also, as I hope this book makes clear, a star, a snatch of dialogue, a dance, a genre, an angle of shot, a face, and many other things. The story is not what happens in a movie, but where the movie's weight lies, the movie's strongest implication. And in any case it is not a matter of anyone believing simply that loneliness is glorious, that women are carnivorous, that nice guys finish last, that appearances are suspicious, that the lynched man is always innocent, that confidence in confidence will see us through, that excess is splendor—to list, in simplified form, only the stories I have looked at in the preceding pages. It is a matter of our feeling that these propositions do get a grip on their subjects, that these stories, with all the necessary reservations and complications and ambivalences, do stake out the territory in question, mark the boundaries of what we think is more or less possible. We can believe or not believe in the propositions. We can disagree and we can quarrel. We can dither; and we can pay very little attention to them at all. They will still be functioning as long as we accept their frames of reference, as long as we feel that these stories offer reasonable versions of what we take life's chances to be, as long as we do not refuse the form in which the debate is cast. Sociologically,

The Wild One (1953): The sociology of cinema—Marlon Brando sets a new style in courtship. Culver Pictures.

it seems to me, we should look for the influence of the movies, not so much in styles of life and upsurges of license and delinquency, as in the pictures of probability that people have, in their sense of the world's workings; in their ideologies, to use a fashionable word. "It is customary to suggest," Louis Althusser writes in *For Marx*,

that ideology belongs to the region of "consciousness". . . . In truth, ideology has very little to do with "consciousness," even supposing this term to have an unambiguous meaning. . . . Ideology is indeed a system of representations, but in the majority of cases these representations have nothing to do with "consciousness": they are usually images and occasionally concepts, but it is above all as *structures* that they impose on the vast majority of men, not via their "consciousness." They are perceived-accepted-suffered cultural objects and they act functionally on men via a process that escapes them. Men "live" their ideologies as the Cartesian "saw" or did not see—if he was not looking at it—the moon two hundred paces away: *not at all as a form of consciousness, but as an object of their "world"*—as their "*world*" itself.

The sociology of American movies thus becomes a question of the contribution of American movies to ideology in Althusser's meaning; of the extent to which the structures of moral and mental life in America, and elsewhere, correspond to structures to be found in films.

Even then it is not a question of the one-way influence of films, but of a complicated transaction, a multiple interplay between films and society. Popular movies take up wishes, dreads, and preoccupations that are loosely (and sometimes not so loosely) scattered about ordinary life, and give them a lodging in fiction, allow them a quick masked passage across our consciousness. But the presence of this material in the movies is a part of its continuing presence in ordinary life too. Movies purvey myths that exist outside the movies, but that also feed on their movie career. The notion that nice guys finish last and the tradition of putting the blame on Mame were not confined to films; but films certainly helped them to stay alive. To be sure, the actual effect of movies, in this sense, seems impossible to determine. But the range and ubiquity of the effect, whatever it is, seems very clear: it is hard to see how anyone could escape the influence of the movies, unless they simply stayed home and talked to no one until they were past being influenced by anything.

This view takes us well beyond America, since American movies at one point, for many people all over the world, *were* the movies: the real thing, pallidly imitated by the cheap local products. In the fifties American films occupied 70 percent of the available projection time in the United Kingdom; 85 percent in the Republic of Ireland; 65 percent in Italy; 60 percent in Mexico. Admittedly these figures represent time on the screen, and give no indication of numbers of people in the audience, or of box office takings; but in a way that makes them all the more impressive, since they mean that newsreels, commercials, and some previews, as well as other main or second features, must have been crowded into the remaining 30 percent (or 15 percent, or 35 or 40 percent) of the screen time.

The movies, then, offered structures of thought and feeling to an almost inconceivable quantity of people, and we live on their legacy in ways we have hardly begun to recognize. I have tried in this book to suggest what that legacy looks like in a few of its different disguises; how it was that movies could matter so much to us even when we didn't give them a second thought—especially when we didn't give them a second thought. But I need to say a word now about why I think the legacy is a legacy, and not a continuing, contemporary relation between ourselves and our films. Of course all kinds of crucial, concrete things happened to the movies in the early sixties: the shrinking of foreign markets; the influx into America of foreign films (942 shown in 1961, as compared with 239 in 1950); the opening of art houses; the growth of independent production; the rise of the producer-director; the appearance of a whole new movie audience, younger, better educated and more discriminating than its predecessor, an audience that treated movies in much the same fashion as an earlier generation had treated jazz. What died in the sixties, to put it all too simply, was the habit of *moviegoing*, the sort of cultural compulsion that took you to the cinema faithfully once or twice every week, whatever was playing.

We lost our myths, it seems, because the mythmaking machinery was getting rusty or was being supplanted by other machinery; and because the old public for them had gone. That sounds right enough, but it leaves some interesting questions up in the air. If we think back to the myths carried by Marilyn Monroe and by Gene Kelly—a devastating innocence and a careering self-confidence—we can see a desperation in them which has very little to do with the shape of the movie industry or the makeup of movie audiences, and everything to do with the way Americans were beginning to see themselves and their country. They are myths that look ill, that look as if their days were numbered. As they were. And not only the days of those particular myths, but the days of full-blown myth itself in the movies.

I don't mean to suggest that the sixties were a decade without myths—I doubt whether any moment in history is without myths—but I do mean to suggest that the sixties were a decade that made life hard for a lot of old stories, an age that was full of an awareness of ugly, unavoidable realities: racism, torture, and assassination; Paris, Prague, Chicago, and the war in Vietnam; drugs, muggings, and turbulent, unmanageable cities. It was not that popular films had suddenly become false, for they had always been false. Just that they had become *too* false, false enough to upset the old, careful truce between wishes and facts. Their mythology was blatant and sentimental, as in Walt Disney; or self-conscious and ironic, as in Robert Aldrich; or it was broken into the smaller, quirkier, personal mythologies of individual directors and writers and producers. Hollywood was still a place (and the studios were far from dead), but it was no longer a style and a world and a national monument. This is not to say we didn't have good, even great, Hollywood films in the sixties, it is to say that these films were different from their ancestors, that they engaged (and failed to engage) reality in new and elusive ways.

In any event, we now look back across the sixties with intense nostalgia, we peer tenderly into the dark on the other side of John Kennedy's death, and this book, of course, is another of those backward glances that have almost come to define the seventies so far. Descendants of Orpheus, forever turning around, we can't take our eyes off the corpses we thought we would bring back from the underworld. For we should be clear what it is we are being nostalgic about when we revisit old Hollywood with such affection. The great days of those films, roughly from 1938 or 1939 to 1962 or 1963, were the days of a precarious balance, since broken, between myth and reality. We relied, so to speak, on the punctuality and discretion of the leopards in Kafka's temple. They were decent enough to keep proper hours, to remain modestly regular in their invasions. Then in the sixties they started to break in at any old time, and the temple was all confusion for a while. Now we are even getting used to the leopards' unreliability, and have our ceremonies ready round the clock. We still do very little about the leopards themselves, of course; they roam the country as before. Our seventies taste for old movies is a variety of yearning not so much for a safer, less threatening America as for an age of more innocent, less strenuous self-deception; an age when the temple was not so busy.

INDEX

Across the Wide Missouri, 129
Adorno, T. W., 19, 170, 173
Adventure, 40, 64
Aldrich, Robert, 84, 195
Alexander the Great, 167, 183
All About Eve, 69, 77, 78, 80, 93
Alloway, Lawrence, 10, 12, 60–61, 62, 110
Allyson, June, 64
Althusser, Louis, 192
Aly Khan, 55, 58, 185
Ameche, Don, 134
America at the Movies (Thorp), 70
American in Paris, An, 100, 148–149, 151, 152–153
Andrews, Dana, 38, 46, 108–109, 137
Anna Karenina, 68
Ariosto, 54
Armstrong, Louis, 152
Astaire, Fred, 11, 56, 147–150, 153, 160, 161, 163, 164
Attendance, 12, 194
Auteur theory, 119
Autobiography (De Mille), 167, 187
Awful Truth, The, 10

Bad and the Beautiful, The, 79
Bad Lands, 132

Balzac, Honoré de, 9
Bancroft, Anne, 134
Band Wagon, The, 147, 151, 153
Banham, Reyner, 9
Barabbas, 167, 177, 178, 186
Barker, Lex, 134
Barthes, Roland, 19
Baxter, Anne, 14, 48, 77
Bazin, André, 6, 13, 119
Behlmer, Rudy, 168
Bellamy, Ralph, 10
Bells Are Ringing, 153
Bendix, William, 32
Ben-Hur, 87, 167, 173, 175, 178, 182, 183
Bergman, Ingrid, 8, 25–26, 27, 67
Berkeley, Busby, 4, 9
Bernhardt, Curtis, 98, 118
Bernstein, Elmer, 175
Best Years of Our Lives, The, 38, 40, 64, 108, 119
Bible, The, 167
Big Sleep, The (Chandler), 102
Big Sleep, The (Hawks), 29, 59, 81, 145
Bishop, Joey, 134
Blackboard Jungle, 127, 151
Blacks, 17–18, 130–134, 136, 143, 145
Blood and Sand, 56
Bloom, Claire, 183

Index

Bluestone, George, 141
Blyth, Ann, 106–107
Boccaccio, 54
Bogart, Humphrey, 8, 24–27, 28–30, 35–36, 38, 40, 43, 66, 67, 163
Bogle, Donald, 134
Boorstin, Daniel, 150–151
Borges, J. L., 119
Boyd, Stephen, 87, 178, 183
Boy Friend, The, 147
Brahm, John, 118
Brando, Marlon, 10, 144, 145, 151–152, 189, 191
Brazzi, Rossano, 130
Brent, George, 4
Broken Arrow, 129
Broken Lance, 131
Brown, Joe E., 162
Bruce, Nigel, 111
Burton, Richard, 14, 175, 176, 183

Cabin in the Sky, 153
Calvet, Corinne, 43, 59
Camille, 68–69
Carey, Gary, 78
Carnegie, Dale, 150
Caron, Leslie, 118
Carson, Jack, 105
Casablanca, 8, 24–27, 38, 40, 43
Cassavetes, John, 132–133
Cavell, Stanley, 42, 101, 116–117, 182
Chambers, Whittaker, 29
Chandler, Jeff, 133–134
Chandler, Raymond, 98, 102
Chaplin, Charles, 6, 161
Charisse, Cyd, 134, 158, 160
Charles, Ray, 95

China, 32
Cincinnati Kid, The, 88, 93–95
Citizen Kane, 10, 13, 117, 124–125
Class, 103, 104, 106–109
Cleopatra, 9, 14, 167, 174, 175–177, 181, 182
Clift, Montgomery, 37, 144, 150, 151
Clockwork Orange, A, 149, 156
Clues, 123–125
Cohn, Harry, 166
Colbert, Claudette, 57
Colman, Ronald, 12
Colorado Territory, 129
Comden, Betty, 154
Confidential Report (*Mr. Arkadin*), 59, 121–122, 124
Conspirator, The, 144
Cook, Elisha, Jr., 81
Cooke, Alistair, 28–29
Cooper, Gary, 36–37, 38, 80, 84–85, 94
Cooper, James Fenimore, 44
Cortez, Stanley, 13
Cotten, Joseph, 118
Cover Girl, 56
Crain, Jeanne, 82, 129, 133–134, 142
Crawford, Broderick, 81–82, 84
Crawford, Joan, 69, 99, 106–107
Croce, Arlene, 148
Cromwell, Richard, 36
Crosby, Bing, 152
Crossfire, 127, 132, 135, 138, 139
Currie, Finlay, 183
Curtis, Tony, 132, 134
Curtiz, Michael, 98, 118

Dailey, Dan, 160
Daisy Kenyon, 69

Dandridge, Dorothy, 129
Dangerous to Know, 77
Daniels, Bebe, 134
Darnell, Linda, 5
David and Bathsheba, 167
Davis, Bette, 69, 104, 106
Day, Doris, 71
Days of Wine and Roses, 127
De Mille, Cecil B., 165–167, 169–171, 173, 176, 177–178, 182, 185–186, 187
Dean, James, 145, 151
Death of a Gunfighter, 129–130
Defiant Ones, The, 111, 132
Del Rio, Dolores, 58, 132
Deming, Barbara, 17, 32, 39–40, 64
Depth of focus, 13, 119
Desnos, Robert, 103
Didion, Joan, 128, 172
Dietrich, Marlene, 7, 8, 12, 58, 69
Disney, Walt, 195
Dmytryk, Edward, 135
Donat, Robert, 114
Donen, Stanley, 154
Donne, John, 11
Double Indemnity, 59, 63
Douglas, Kirk, 79, 183
Dunne, John Gregory, 133
Durkheim, Emile, 20
Durocher, Leo, 76
Dylan, Bob, 182

East of Eden, 151
Eddy, Nelson, 148
Edge of the City, 17, 132–133
Edwards, Blake, 116
Egyptian, The, 167
Eisenhower, Dwight D., 39, 161, 162, 163

El Cid, 174, 183
Eliot, George, 11
Emerson, Ralph Waldo, 122, 124
Epic spectacles, 165–188
Everson, William K., 10, 47, 88
Every Night at Eight, 147
Experiment in Terror, 116

Fairy tales, 104, 108–110, 127
Fall of the Roman Empire, The, 167, 178, 183
Fallen Sparrow, The, 10
Far Country, The, 43
Farouk, King, 185
Fastest Gun Alive, The, 81–84
Fellini, Federico, 11
Fenin, George N., 10, 47, 88
Ferrer, Mel, 134, 142
Fields, W. C., 68
Films noirs, 97–115
Fitzgerald, F. Scott, 172–173
Flying Down to Rio, 149
Flynn, Errol, 12
Focus, depth of, 13, 119
Fonda, Henry, 46
Fontaine, Joan, 63, 111–112, 115
For Marx (Althusser), 192
For Me and My Gal, 4, 6, 18
Ford, Glenn, 33, 52, 54, 55, 56, 67, 80, 81–84, 150, 151
Ford, John, 10, 46
Foreign films, 194
Frazer, J. G., 88
Freed, Arthur, 147, 154
French, Philip, 22, 43, 48, 84, 87. 166
Freud, Sigmund, 38, 144
Friar, Natasha, 134
Friar, Ralph, 134

Index

From Here to Eternity, 37
From Reverence to Rape (Haskell), 70, 128
Fury, 136

Guinness, Alec, 183
Gunfighter, The, 87
Gunfights, 81–87, 96
Gunga Din, 10
Guys and Dolls, 151

Gable, Clark, 34, 35, 189–190
Gangster movies, 47, 93
Garbo, Greta, 57, 69
Gardner, Ava, 58, 62
Garfield, John, 39–40, 41
Garland, Judy, 6, 9
Garson, Greer, 64, 71
Gaynor, Mitzi, 130
Generation on Trial, A (Cooke), 28–29
Genn, Leo, 183
German directors, 118
Geronimo, 10, 132
Giant, 95, 132, 174, 175
Gidget, 69
Gigi, 69
Gilda, 51–56, 61, 69
Gili, Jean, 48
Gleason, Jackie, 90–94
Goddard, Paulette, 134
Golden Bough (Frazer), 88
Gone With The Wind, 6, 8, 9, 12, 13–14, 33–35, 69, 141, 168, 180
Goulding, Edmund, 4
Gow, Gordon, 143
Grable, Betty, 58
Grant, Cary, 10, 16, 18, 111–112, 114, 115, 116
Greatest Story Ever Told, The, 167, 177, 183
Green, Adolph, 154
Greenberg, Joel, 63, 98, 102, 135
Greenstreet, Sidney, 26–27
Guess Who's Coming to Dinner, 128

Hackett, Buddy, 134
Harder They Fall, The, 66, 77–78
Harriet Craig, 69
Harrison, Rex, 14, 175, 187
Hartz, Louis, 46
Haskell, Molly, 70, 72, 128
Hathaway, Henry, 36
Havilland, Olivia de, 13–14, 34
Haymes, Dick, 58
Hayworth, Rita, 12, 51–66, 68, 71, 74
Hecht, Ben, 173, 174, 177, 183, 187
Henreid, Paul, 26, 104, 106
Hepburn, Audrey, 134
Heston, Charlton, 87, 174, 177, 183, 187
High Society, 152
Higham, Charles, 10, 13, 63, 98, 102, 135.
His Girl Friday, 10
Hiss, Alger, 29, 164
Hitchcock, Alfred, 6, 100–101, 111, 112, 114, 116, 120, 121, 122–124
Holden, William, 35–36, 134, 150, 151, 162
Hollywood (Rosten), 22
Hollywood in the Forties (Higham and Greenberg), 63, 98
Hollywood Musical, The (Russell Taylor), 153
Home of the Brave, 131

Homosexuality, 132–133
Horkheimer, Max, 19, 170, 173
Horne, Lena, 130
House of Strangers, 131
Howard, Leslie, 12, 34
Howe, James Wong, 13
Hudson, Rock, 67, 134
Hunchback of Notre Dame, The, 10
Hunter, Jeffrey, 134
Hustler, The, 66, 88–95
Huston, John, 144

I'll Cry Tomorrow, 127
Image, The (Boorstin), 150–151
Indians, American, 129, 131–135
Individualism, 28, 31–33
Informer, The, 131
Inherit the Wind, 111
Innocence of victims, 135–145
Isolationism, 25–31
It's Always Fair Weather, 150, 151,
   153, 154, 158–163
Ivy, 63, 64

James, Henry, 31, 35
Jefferson, Thomas, 30
Jews, 131, 132, 135–136, 138, 184
Jezebel, 69
Joseph and His Brethren, 166, 168
Joyce, James, 113
Judgment at Nuremberg, 111, 128
Julius Caesar, 10

Kael, Pauline, 125, 130, 133, 136,
   138, 141

Kafka, Franz, 18, 145, 163–164,
   194, 195
Kelly, Gene, 4, 6, 9, 18, 147–161
Kelly, Grace, 58, 152
Kerr, Deborah, 175, 183
Kerr, John, 130
Khartoum, 174, 183
Killers, 80–82, 84–87
Killers, The, 60–61
King of Kings, 167
Kirk, G. S., 21
Knox, Donald, 100
Kramer, Stanley, 111, 128, 131
Kubrick, Stanley, 149

Ladd, Alan, 32, 35–36
Lady from Shanghai, 59–62, 117
Lady and the Tramp, The, 40
Lady Vanishes, The, 116, 122–123
Lamarr, Hedy, 167
Lambert, Gavin, 6
Lancaster, Burt, 84
Land of the Pharaohs, 167
Lang, Fritz, 118
Lanza, Mario, 148
Laramie, 10
Last of the Comanches, The, 44
Last Frontier, The, 44
Last Roundup, The, 44
Last Tycoon, The (Fitzgerald), 173
Last Wagon, The, 44
Lasky, Jesse L., Jr., 186
Laura, 69
Laurentiis, Dino de, 173–174
Laurents, Arthur, 131
Laurie, Piper, 66, 68, 90, 92
Law, 46–47
Law and Jake Wade, The, 43–45
Lawrence, D. H., 11

Index

Lawrence of Arabia, 174
Leave Her to Heaven, 63
Leigh, Vivien, 6, 8, 13–14, 34–35
Lemmon, Jack, 72, 162
Lévi-Strauss, Claude, 20
Liberal Tradition in America, The (Hartz), 46
Limelight, 6
Little Sister, The (Chandler), 102
Lives of a Bengal Lancer, 36–37, 132
Lockwood, Margaret, 123
Logan, Joshua, 162
Lolita, 69
Loneliness, 25–29, 43, 50, 163
Loren, Sophia, 183
Lost Boundaries, 134
Lost Man, The, 131
Lost Patrol, 132
Lost Weekend, The, 64, 127
Love Happy, 72
Lubitsch, Ernst, 11
Lugosi, Bela, 134
Lynching, 135–141

Macdonald, Ross, 102
Macready, George, 52, 54, 56, 67
Magic Factory, The (Knox), 100
Magnificent Ambersons, The, 10
Maltese Falcon, The, 29
Mamoulian, Rouben, 4
Man Who Knew Too Much, The, 101
Man With the Cloak, The, 118
Man With the Golden Arm, The, 127
Mankiewicz, Joseph L., 14, 78, 80, 131, 175, 177
Mann, Anthony, 43, 178
Mann, Thomas, 166, 168
Mansfield, Jayne, 58
Marin, Edward L., 99

Mark, The, 133, 136
Mark of Zorro, The, 3–5, 8–9
Markle, Fletcher, 118
Marques, Maria Elena, 129
Marty, 19
Marx, Groucho, 10, 72
Mary of Scotland, 10
Mature, Victor, 167
Mayer, L. B., 166, 167, 168
Mayersberg, Paul, 13, 111
Mayo, Virginia, 129
McCarthy, Joseph, 77, 140, 164
McCrea, Joel, 129
McLaglen, Andrew, 67
McQueen, Butterfly, 107
McQueen, Steve, 94–95
McVay, Douglas, 153
Meet Me in St. Louis, 147, 153
Memo from David O. Selznick (Behlmer), 168
Michelangelo, 177
Mifune, Toshiro, 133
Mildred Pierce, 69, 98–99, 104, 105, 106–107
Miller, Ann, 155
Miller, Arthur, 13
Mills, C. Wright, 181
Minnelli, Vincente, 79
Mirrors, 117, 118, 120–121
Miscegenation, 129–130
Misfits, The, 59, 72
Mr. Arkadin (Confidential Report), 59, 121–122, 124
Mitchell, Margaret, 34, 35
Mitchum, Robert, 35–36
Modern Times, 6, 161
Monroe, Marilyn, 56, 65, 71–74, 143, 194
Movie Moguls, The (French), 22
Munshin, Jules, 155
Musical Film, The (McVay), 153
Musicals, 100, 127, 146–164

Mythological function of movies, 20–23, 194–195

New York Review of Books, The, 172
Newman, Paul, 66, 67, 80, 89, 90–93
Night and Day, 16, 18
Night Song, 104, 108–110
Ninotchka, 69
Nixon, Richard M., 31
No Way Out, 127
Nocturne, 99–100
Nora Prentiss, 69
North by Northwest, 114, 116
Novak, Kim, 71, 162
Now Voyager, 104, 106
Nuyen, France, 130

Oberon, Merle, 4, 63, 108–109
O'Connor, Donald, 156, 158, 160
Odd Man Out, 131
Of Human Bondage, 69
Oliver!, 147
Olivier, Laurence, 178, 183
On the Beach, 111
On the Town, 147, 154–155, 158
On the Waterfront, 151
Only Angels Have Wings, 56
Only Good Indian, The (Friar and Friar), 134
Ormandy, Eugene, 109
Out of the Past, 61
Overblown movies, 3–15
Ox-Bow Incident, The, 16, 46, 135, 136, 137, 138, 141

Paget, Debra, 129
Palance, Jack, 177
Parker, Eleanor, 41
Parks, Larry, 134
Pearson, Beatrice, 134
Peck, Gregory, 48
Perelman, S. J., 134
Phantom Lady, 102
Philadelphia Story, The, 152
Picnic, 151, 162–163
Picture (Ross), 22
Pinky, 127, 129
Place in the Sun, A, 151
Plainsman, The, 10
Plummer, Christopher, 178, 183
Poe, Edgar Allan, 118
Poitier, Sidney, 17–18, 132, 133, 143
Popcorn Venus (Rosen), 64
Porter, Cole, 16, 64, 152
Possessed, 98, 101
Postman Always Rings Twice, The, 63
Power, Tyrone, 3–5, 8–9
Preminger, Otto, 118
Previn, André, 158
Pride of the Marines, 39–40, 41, 64, 108
Problem movies, 127–145
Proust, Marcel, 66

Queen Christina, 68
Quo Vadis?, 10, 167, 175, 177, 178, 183

Race, 17–18, 129–136, 143, 145
Raft, George, 99

Index

Rains, Claude, 8, 25, 26, 27, 43
Rebecca, 69
Rebel Without a Cause, 151
Redgrave, Michael, 123
Reflections, 117, 118, 120–121
Repetition in movies, 9–10
Resentment against others, 32–33
Return to Paradise, 37
Revel, Jean-François, 38
Reynolds, Debbie, 156
Rhapsody in Blue, 141
Riesman, David, 143, 149
Riesman, Evelyn T., 143
Robe, The, 167, 183
Roberta, 69
Robertson, Dale, 86
Robinson, David, 19
Robinson, Edward G., 93–95, 122, 180
Rogers, Ginger, 147, 148, 149, 153
Rosen, Marjorie, 64, 68, 72
Ross, Lillian, 11, 22
Rossen, Robert, 66, 90, 92
Rosten, Leo, 22
Rousseau, Jean Jacques, 30, 31
Rovere, Richard, 77
Rozsa, Miklos, 175
Running Away From Myself (Deming), 17, 39–40
Russell, Jane, 58
Russell, Rosalind, 162
Russell Taylor, John, 153
Ryan, Robert, 138, 139

Samson and Delilah, 167, 178, 179
Sanders, George, 77
Scarlet Pimpernel, The, 12
Scarlet Street, 63
Schulberg, Budd, 79

Scott, George C., 66, 67, 90–92
Scott, Randolph, 47, 49
Scott, Zachary, 105, 107
Selfishness, 27, 28, 32–39, 50
Selznick, David O., 34, 35, 167–168, 173, 185
Set-Up, The, 95
Shall We Dance, 161
Shatner, William, 134
Sheepman, The, 33
Ship of Fools, 128
Simmons, Jean, 183
Simonci, Louis, 81
Sinatra, Frank, 152, 155
Singin' in the Rain, 147, 151, 154, 155–158, 160, 161
Siodmak, Robert, 102, 118
Sloane, Everett, 60
Slouching Towards Bethlehem (Didion), 128
Snake Pit, The, 128
So Evil My Love, 63
Social class, 103, 104, 106–109
Sodom and Gomorrah, 167
Some Like It Hot, 72, 73, 162
Son of Kong, 10
Song to Remember, A, 141
Sound of Music, The, 147
South Pacific, 130
Spartacus, 167, 183
Spellbound, 64
Spoilers, The, 47
Sports, 88–95
Stagecoach, 10
Stanwyck, Barbara, 63, 68, 110
Steiger, Rod, 66, 77–78
Stella Dallas, 69
Sterling, Jan, 66, 68
Sternberg, Joseph von, 12
Stevens, George, 174
Stewart, James, 43, 48
Strange Love of Martha Ivers, The, 63

Stranger, The, 122, 124
Strangers on a Train, 116
Stroheim, Erich von, 11
Studio, The (Dunne), 133
Sturges, John, 43
Success, 76–80, 86, 88, 90–95
Suckow, Ruth, 58
Sunset Boulevard, 59, 69
Susan Lenox, 68
Suspicion, 111–112, 113, 114, 115

Trial, The (Kafka), 145
Trotti, Lamar, 16, 46
Try and Get Me, 136
Turner, Lana, 63

Undefeated, The, 67
Unsuspected, The, 98, 101
Uptight, 131
Ustinov, Peter, 183

Tamiroff, Akim, 77
Taylor, Elizabeth, 14, 151, 175
Taylor, Robert, 43–45, 134, 144, 175, 183
Temptation, 63
Ten Commandments, The, 14, 165–166, 167, 170, 171, 173, 175, 177–178, 183, 185, 186, 187
Thalberg, Irving, 172–173
They Won't Forget, 136
Thirty-nine Steps, The, 114
Thomas, Bob, 10, 56
Thomas, J. Parnell, 140
Thoroughly Modern Millie, 69
Thorp, Margaret, 23, 70
Those Endearing Young Charms, 40
Thrillers, 97–124
Thucydides, 150
Thundering Herd, The, 10
Tierney, Gene, 63
Till We Meet Again, 4, 9
Todd, Ann, 63
Toland, Gregg, 13
Toms, Coons, Mulattoes, Mammies, and Bucks (Bogle), 134
Tone, Franchot, 36
Top Hat, 148
Touch of Evil, 7, 8

Van Upp, Virginia, 55
Vanity Fair (Thackeray), 34
Veblen, Thorstein, 170, 181
Veidt, Conrad, 27
Vera Cruz, 84–86, 94
Vera-Ellen, 158
Victims, innocence of, 135–145
Vidor, Charles, 52
Violent America (Alloway), 12, 60–61
Visual effects, 97–125

Wagner, Robert, 134
War Lord, The, 174
War and Peace (Tolstoy), 177
Washington, George, 30
Wayne, John, 47, 49, 67, 134
Weld, Tuesday, 94
Welles, Orson, 6, 7, 8, 58, 59, 60, 61, 63, 117, 120, 121–122, 124–125
Wellman, William, 135
West, Nathanael, 16

Index

Western, Le, 48, 81
Westerns, 44–50, 81–88, 96
What Makes Sammy Run? (Schulberg), 79
Whatever Happened to Hollywood? (Lasky), 186
Whitman, Stuart, 135–136
Whitty, Dame May, 122–123
Who's Afraid of Virginia Woolf?, 69
Widmark, Richard, 44, 45, 129–130
Wild One, The, 127, 144, 151–152, 191
Wilder, Billy, 59, 118
Wilson, Woodrow, 30–31
Winters, Shelley, 151
Wizard of Oz, The, 153
Woman in the Window, 63
Women, 26, 42–43, 51–74, 162–163

World Viewed, The (Cavell), 42
Wuthering Heights (Brontë), 34
Wuthering Heights (Wyler), 141
Wyler, William, 87, 119, 167, 173
Wyman, Jane, 64

Yellow Sky, 48
You Were Never Lovelier, 56
You'll Never Get Rich, 56
Young, Loretta, 32, 122
Young, Robert, 138

Zanuck, Darryl F., 128
Zanuck, Richard, 133
Zinnemann, Fred, 118, 133, 134